SIMPLY SWEET
NOSTALGIC BAKES

SIMPLY SWEET NOSTALGIC BAKES

55 Elegant Takes on Comfort Classics

EMMA DUCKWORTH

Creator of Emma Duckworth Bakes

PAGE STREET
PUBLISHING CO.

PAGE STREET
PUBLISHING CO.

First published in 2021 by
Page Street Publishing Co.
27 Congress Street, Suite 105
Salem, MA 01970
www.pagestreetpublishing.com

Distributed by Macmillan, sales in Canada by The Canadian Manda Group.

25   24   23   22   21   1   2   3   4   5

ISBN-13: 978-1-64567-408-5
ISBN-10: 1-64567-408-8

Library of Congress Control Number: 2021931351

Cover and book design by Kylie Alexander for Page Street Publishing Co.
Photography by Emma Duckworth

Printed and bound in China

DEDICATION

This book is dedicated to my family. Coco, Lani, Malia and Anthony,
I quite literally could not have written and produced this without you.
It was a team effort!

For the cake makers and dessert lovers out there, I hope that this cookbook
takes you down memory lane and reminds you of some delicious treats that
you've enjoyed in your past. It thrills me to be able to share my recipes with
you and show the influences of my life in the baking within these pages.

CONTENTS

INTRODUCTION

For me, baking has always brought with it a deeper level of comfort than other types of cooking. Why is that? I think because whether it's through taste, through smell or even through touch, baked goods can evoke a memory that connects you with your past. We all have intricately layered lives that evolve over the years to create a textured and meaningful connection to who and how we are in the kitchen.

I had an incredibly different childhood compared to most. My family spent time as expatriates in Asia, and throughout my childhood I was lucky enough to live in the Philippines, China and India. You can imagine how spending so much time in far-away countries such as these allowed me to develop my love and appreciation for Asian flavors. Kaffir lime leaves, lemongrass, fennel seeds, saffron, star anise, coconut and sweet mango, to name a few flavors, have always played a part in my development as a home cook and baker.

With an English dad and French mum, I've also been able to forge lasting connections with these countries and beyond. Food at home was always interesting and flavor packed, as my mum is a fantastic cook. Dad traveled a lot for work at the time, so it was Mum's exploration into a vast variety of flavors that expanded my palate at home. However, being French, we always had a connection with this beautiful European country. Crêpes were eaten at home regularly, and it's a tradition that I have continued on with my kids. (In fact, I don't think I had an American-style pancake until we holidayed in Florida when I was ten years old.) Through my connection with my French heritage and many trips to France, I've had a love affair with French pastries for much of my life. Each one, whether a macaron, an éclair or a perfect slice of tarte Tatin will transport me back to a specific time and place where I've enjoyed it.

Australia also holds a very special place in my heart. Life took me from boarding school in Cheltenham to university in Oxford (no not at THE university!) to studying design in London. And from there, I traveled to Australia with my best friend for a gap year. Little did I know that this decision would change my life. On the sunny shores of Manly Beach in Sydney, I met Anthony, a surf-loving local boy. Fast-forward eighteen years, and we have three incredible girls, Malia, Lani and Coco, and a beautiful fifteen years spent in Sydney. During these years, my love of tropical flavors like pineapple, mango and passion fruit grew. Pavlova became a must at most gatherings, and I learned about friands and lamingtons.

I've led a very internationally rich life, having spent so much of my time overseas, and it doesn't go past me just how lucky I am. Having moved back to London into the leafy suburb of Chiswick with my family, I've had the opportunity to develop my love of baking and a passion for photography into a "living." I get to think about sweet treats and desserts all day, every day, coming up with new recipes to share with family and friends.

When I think of recipes that hold a special place in my heart, they invariably stem from a memory. I believe that our life is broken down into a multitude of personal and individual experiences that together form the pages of nostalgia within ourselves. It's this trip down memory lane and flashbacks into our past that provide the foundation for who we are as bakers. Whether it's the blueberry pie that smells like time spent in your nan's kitchen, the mango froyo that takes you back to sand-filled beach days or an éclair that reminds you of trips to the South of France, food has the ability to provide comfort. From these memories we can expand our own repertoire of recipes that can be passed down from generation to generation.

This is why this cookbook holds such a special place in my heart. It's given me the ability to share with you old-fashioned bakes, retro classics and nostalgic comfort food while giving them an Emma-like reinvented twist. A modern take through new flavor combinations such as chocolate and rosemary (page 73), orange blossom and thyme (page 19) and apple and fennel (page 60), that will entice you into the kitchen. Having said that, there are some classics that are perfect the way they are, like alfajores (page 23), blondies (page 27) and Black Forest cake (page 94).

During the concept-development stage of this book, when I thought about recipes that meant something to me, my page was filled with diverse ideas including cookies, fudge, danish pastries, madeleines, lemon drizzle cake, arctic roll, truffles, French apple tart, banoffee pie and steamed pudding, to name a few. From there, I was able to separate these goodies into six chapters: cookies, brownies and slices, pies and tarts, cakes, puddings, snacks and sweet pastries and frozen treats. Within each chapter I then expanded on my favorite nostalgic sweet treats and desserts, finalizing a list that I believe will touch the hearts of many.

My hope is that you'll flip through this book, a cup of tea in hand, and stumble across recipes that instantly spark a memory, make you feel like a kid again or wrap a cloak of familiarity around you.

I dream that over the coming years, this cookbook becomes dog-eared and stained with ingredients through use. Mark it with personal notes, allow the kids to riffle through it, bookmark favorite recipes. The fact that my recipes can become a small part of your baking exploration, in your home, with your family and friends, fills me with endless amounts of joy.

E. Duckworth.

SCRUMPTIOUS COOKIES, BROWNIES AND SLICES

A very sweet way to start the book is with a chapter filled with cookies, brownies and slices. This chapter is full of instantly recognizable sweet treats that we know and love, but I've added my own spin with interesting flavor twists throughout these pages. And for those wondering what a "slice" is, I classify it as those delicious treats that are put together with various layers in a baking pan and then sliced into individual portions. Espresso Millionaire Shortbread Bars (page 28) are a perfect example of a slice.

Chocolate chip cookies have been given a rich, flavorful upgrade and become Spelt Walnut Chocolate Chunk Cookies (page 13). Rich, indulgent, fudgy Tahini-Swirled Dark Chocolate Brownies (page 24) have the surprise addition of sesame brittle broken throughout, and Espresso Millionaire Shortbread Bars (page 28) are elevated to a thing of beauty with the addition of espresso in the caramel.

The Take-Me-Back Wagon Wheel Slice (page 31) reminds me of childhood days squishing out marshmallow between buttery, crumbly shortbread, licking sticky fingers when finished. It sits alongside a group of recipes that would be great to please a crowd. Bake them, slice them, box them and bring them with you to a party or an outdoor gathering, and you'll make a lot of people very happy!

SPELT WALNUT CHOCOLATE CHUNK COOKIES

Yield: **24-30** *cookies*

As far as nostalgic baking goes, chocolate chip cookies sit firmly in the Nostalgia Hall of Fame. Whether you enjoyed homemade or store-bought cookies, it's safe to say we've all loved a chocolate chip cookie or two. To elevate these cookies, I've browned the butter and added spelt flour to the batter, which gives a slightly nuttier flavor, and paired with walnuts, which complement the caramel notes of the brown sugar. Instead of chocolate chips, I've used chocolate chunks, so when baked, the cookies have crisp edges but soft gooey centers with molten chocolate puddles. It's impossible to eat just one!

1 cup plus 2 tbsp (260 g) unsalted butter, room temperature

1 cup (220 g) firmly packed light brown sugar

2 large eggs, room temperature

1 tsp vanilla extract

1½ cups (190 g) spelt flour

1 cup plus 2 tbsp (140 g) all-purpose flour

1 tsp cornstarch

1 tsp baking powder

1 tsp baking soda

½ tsp salt

1 cup (150 g) coarsely chopped 70% dark chocolate

1 cup (150 g) coarsely chopped milk chocolate

⅔ cup (80 g) coarsely chopped walnuts

1 tsp natural sea salt flakes, for sprinkling on top

Tip: Two minutes before baking has finished, add a couple extra pieces of chocolate onto the top of each cookie for those delectable chocolate puddles.

Start by browning the butter. In a small saucepan over medium heat, melt the butter. Continue to cook until the butter is golden brown and has a nutty fragrance, about 4 to 5 minutes. The butter turns very quickly from golden to burnt, so keep an eye on it. Once golden brown, remove the butter from the heat and measure out 1 cup (240 ml), getting all the brown bits in there. Allow to cool for 10 minutes or until at room temperature.

In the bowl of an electric stand mixer fitted with the paddle attachment, cream the browned butter and sugar on medium speed for 5 minutes, or until pale. Reduce the speed to low and add the eggs one at a time and the vanilla, beating well after each addition until well incorporated. Scrape down the sides and bottom of the bowl. In a separate bowl, sift the spelt flour, all-purpose flour, cornstarch, baking powder, baking soda and salt, and stir to combine. Add the prepared flour mix, dark and milk chocolates and walnuts to the bowl of the stand mixer and beat on low until just combined.

Preheat the oven to 350°F (180°C). Line a baking sheet with parchment paper.

Using a cookie scoop or a tablespoon, scoop balls of cookie dough into 1-inch (2.5-cm) balls and place on the prepared tray. Place the tray in the fridge for 45 minutes (or the freezer for 20 minutes) to rest. Remove the cookie dough balls from the fridge and place on two lined room-temperature baking sheets, leaving a good 2 inches (5 cm) between the balls. Bake for 10 to 12 minutes, until the edges are just turning golden. If you prefer crisper cookies, add a couple of extra minutes or so to the cooking time. Remove the trays from the oven and sprinkle each cookie with sea salt flakes. Leave the cookies on the baking sheet for 15 minutes to cool, and then transfer to a wire rack to cool further. Cookies can be stored at room temperature or in the fridge for up to 3 days in an airtight container, or in the freezer for up to 3 months.

LEMON ROSE SHORTBREAD WEDGES

Yield: **12** *slices*

Shortbread biscuits are a staple of any biscuit tin in England. I fondly remember delving into my Nana's tin for a sugary piece of shortbread every time we visited. Buttery, crumbly and sweet, they are traditionally made with butter, sugar and flour, but my take adds the subtle flavoring of dried rose petals paired with a tangy lemon icing. By making it in a tart pan as a round and cutting it into wedges for simplicity, I've taken this humble biscuit and turned it into a real teatime treat.

For the Shortbread

1 cup (230 g) unsalted butter, room temperature

¾ cup (150 g) granulated sugar

2 tbsp (2 g) finely crushed dried rose petals

2¾ cups (345 g) all-purpose flour, plus more for kneading

¼ tsp salt

For the Lemon Glaze

1 cup (120 g) confectioners' sugar

Zest of 1 large lemon

2 tbsp (30 ml) fresh lemon juice, plus more as needed

1 tbsp (1 g) dried rose petals, to decorate

Tips: This makes a thick shortbread wedge. If you prefer thinner wedges, split the dough in half and press it into two 6-inch (15-cm) cake pans or springform pans. Keep an eye on your cooking time, as they will require only about 20 to 25 minutes to bake.

The rose flavor from the rose petals is subtle. If you prefer a stronger rose flavor, add ½ to 1 teaspoon of rose extract into the dough along with the rose petals.

Preheat the oven to 325°F (165°C). Grease a 9-inch (23-cm) shallow fluted tart pan with a removable base (or alternatively, use a cake pan with a removable base), and line it with a circle of parchment paper cut to size.

To make the shortbread, in the bowl of an electric stand mixer fitted with the paddle attachment, cream the butter, sugar and rose petals together on medium speed for 5 minutes, or until pale. Scrape down the sides of the bowl. Add the flour and salt and mix until the dough just comes together.

Turn out onto a lightly floured countertop and knead with floured hands for 2 minutes until the dough is smooth. Press together with your hands until a cohesive dough is formed. Place the dough into the prepared tart pan and with the palm of your hand, smooth the dough right to the edge of the pan all the way around. Using the flat base of a glass measuring cup, smooth it out further. Use your fingertips to create indents all the way around the edge, if desired. Cut the dough into wedges using a sharp knife, and then, using a bamboo skewer or the tines of a fork, neatly poke 5 to 6 holes into each wedge. Bake for 30 to 35 minutes, or until the edges start to turn golden. Remove from the oven and allow to cool in the tart pan for 10 minutes, and then recut the wedges. Leave the shortbread to cool completely in the pan before removing.

To make the glaze, use a fine-mesh sieve to sift the confectioners' sugar into a medium mixing bowl. Add the lemon zest and whisk in the lemon juice until you have a smooth, thick glaze. If the glaze is too thick, add more lemon juice, 1 teaspoon at a time, until you've reached your desired consistency. Spoon the glaze over the shortbread wedges and sprinkle with dried rose petals to decorate. I crush half of the rose petals so that there is a variation in size. Set aside for 15 minutes, or until the glaze has completely set before serving.

Shortbread can be stored at room temperature in an airtight container for up to 1 week or in the freezer for 3 to 4 weeks.

CRANBERRY, PISTACHIO AND WHITE CHOCOLATE BISCOTTI

Yield: **25–30** *biscotti*

I've been lucky enough to travel to Italy quite a few times, and my favorite biscuits that I've eaten there are almond biscotti. I can picture myself sitting by the Trevi Fountain in Rome, soaking in the beauty all around while biting into a crunchy, twice-baked biscotto. My version of this delightful treat combines cranberries and pistachio with a hint of orange in the dough. Once baked, they're drizzled with white chocolate and sprinkled with more pistachios, making them ready to be enjoyed alongside an espresso. These make a wonderfully festive gift at Christmas time but can be enjoyed all year round!

For the Biscotti

1 cup (200 g) granulated sugar, plus 1 tsp extra for sprinkling

Zest of 1 large orange

¼ cup (60 g) unsalted butter, room temperature

3 large eggs, room temperature, divided

1 tsp vanilla extract

1¾ cups (220 g) all-purpose flour

½ tsp baking powder

½ tsp salt

¾ cup (90 g) coarsely chopped unsalted pistachios

⅔ cup (80 g) dried cranberries

1 tbsp (15 ml) milk

To make the biscotti, in a small bowl, combine the sugar and orange zest, and using your fingertips, rub the two together for 1 minute to release the oils of the zest into the sugar. In the bowl of an electric stand mixer fitted with the paddle attachment, cream the butter and sugar-zest mixture together on medium speed for 5 minutes, or until pale. Reduce the speed to low and add 2 of the eggs, one at a time, and the vanilla, beating well after each addition until well incorporated. Scrape the sides and bottom of the bowl.

In a separate bowl, sift the flour, baking powder and salt, and then stir to combine. Add the prepared flour mix, pistachios and cranberries to the mixing bowl and combine on low speed until just combined. Cover the dough and refrigerate for 1 hour.

Preheat the oven to 350°F (180°C), and line a large baking sheet with parchment paper.

(continued)

For the Topping

1⅓ cups (200 g) coarsely chopped white chocolate

2 tbsp (15 g) finely chopped shelled pistachios

Remove the biscotti dough from the fridge and divide it in half. Using floured or moistened hands, shape each half into a 12 x 2–inch (30 x 5–cm) log on the baking sheet. Leave space between the logs, as the dough will spread while baking. Make an egg wash by whisking together the remaining egg and milk in a small bowl. Brush the egg wash over the logs, and then sprinkle them with the extra teaspoon of granulated sugar. Bake the biscotti for about 20 to 25 minutes, or until firm and golden. Remove from the oven and set aside to cool for 10 minutes. Reduce the heat to 275°F (135°C). After 10 minutes, using a serrated knife, cut the logs diagonally into ¾-inch (2-cm) slices. Place the slices on their sides on the parchment-covered baking sheet. Bake the biscotti for 15 to 20 minutes, or until dry and crisp, turning halfway through the baking time. Allow them to cool fully. Once cooled, there will still be a little give in the biscotti. If you want very dry, hard biscotti, add another 10 or so minutes to the bake time.

To make the topping, melt the white chocolate in a bowl over a pan of simmering water, ensuring the bottom of the bowl does not come into contact with the water. Once melted, remove from the heat and dip the end of each biscotti or drizzle chocolate over each before placing them back onto the baking sheet. Sprinkle pistachios over the white chocolate. Place the baking sheet into the fridge for 10 minutes to help the white chocolate set.

Biscotti can be stored at room temperature in an airtight container for up to 2 weeks or in the freezer for 3 months. Place parchment paper between the layers of biscotti to protect the white chocolate.

Tip: I suggest dipping biscotti in warm coffee or hot chocolate to serve!

ORANGE BLOSSOM THYME MADELEINES

Yield: **12** *large madeleines (or 24 small)*

In France, madeleines are as popular an afternoon treat for *un quatre-heures* (a snack for after school) as shortbread is in England. I didn't learn to make them until a couple of years ago, as I'd foolishly put them into the "too difficult basket." I was so wrong. Once you have the know-how, you'll find these surprisingly easy to make. With their distinct shell-shaped design, these small, classic French sponges are incredibly light in texture with their tender crumb. I've combined the summery flavors of fragrant orange blossom and delicate thyme so that they are light in taste, too.

For the Madeleines

½ cup (115 g) unsalted butter, plus 1 tbsp (15 g) to grease the mold

½ cup (100 g) granulated sugar

Zest of 2 large oranges

2 large eggs, room temperature

1 tbsp (15 ml) honey

2 tsp (10 ml) orange blossom water

1 tsp vanilla extract

1 cup (125 g) all-purpose flour

1 tsp baking powder

¼ tsp salt

1 tbsp (2 g) roughly chopped fresh thyme leaves, plus extra for topping

To make the madeleines, in a small saucepan over medium heat, melt the butter. Once fully melted, pour the butter into a bowl, set aside and allow it to come to room temperature. In a small bowl, combine the sugar and orange zest and using your fingertips, rub them together for 1 minute to release the oils of the zest into the sugar. In the bowl of an electric stand mixer fitted with the whisk attachment, place the eggs, sugar and orange zest, honey, orange blossom water and vanilla, and whip on high for 5 minutes until the mixture is thick and pale.

Sift the flour, baking powder and salt into the egg batter, and mix on low until the flour mixture is no longer visible. Add the thyme leaves, drizzle the melted butter down the side of the bowl and gently fold together. Take care not to overmix or you may lose the volume of the whisked eggs. Cover with plastic wrap and refrigerate for 3 hours to let the batter rest (or overnight if preferred). The resting time allows the signature bump to form when baking.

Preheat the oven to 350°F (180°C) about 30 minutes before baking. Using a pastry brush, generously brush melted butter into the molds of your madeleine pan, and dust with a little flour, knocking out the excess. Place the pan into the fridge until ready to use.

(continued)

For the Orange Glaze

1½ cups (180 g) confectioners' sugar

2 tbsp (30 ml) fresh orange juice, plus more as needed

Once the oven is at temperature, remove the batter from the fridge. Divide the batter equally between each shell mold. Don't level the batter out. Bake the madeleines for 10 to 12 minutes, rotating the pan after 8 minutes. They are ready when the "humps" have risen, and they are browned on the edges. Remove the madeleines from the oven and allow them to cool in the pan for a couple of minutes. Give the pans a little jiggle and the madeleines should pop out. If they stick, run a knife around the edges to loosen them. Allow them to cool fully on a wire rack.

To make the orange glaze, use a fine-mesh sieve to sift the confectioners' sugar into a medium mixing bowl. Whisk in the orange juice until you have a smooth, thick glaze. If the glaze is too thick, add more orange juice or water, 1 teaspoon at a time, until you've reached your desired consistency.

To assemble, place a cooling rack over a sheet of parchment paper. Dip the bottom half of the shell (the non-hump side) into the orange glaze. Transfer the coated madeleine to the cooling rack, hump-side down, allowing the excess glaze to drip off. Decorate with extra thyme leaves. Repeat this process with the rest of the madeleines. Allow the glaze to set for 5 to 10 minutes before serving.

Madeleines are best eaten on the same day but can be stored in an airtight container at room temperature for up to 2 days.

Tip: If you don't own a large shell madeleines pan, a standard madeleines pan can be used. This batter will produce 24 smaller madeleines and the cooking time should be reduced to 8 to 9 minutes.

COCONUT DULCE DE LECHE ALFAJORES

Yield: **18–20** *sandwich cookies*

I've been seeing these South American cookies on the internet for years and, for millions, these well-known sandwich cookies hold a very special place in their hearts. With this recipe, I haven't deviated from tradition, as these crumbly, shortbread cookies filled with a luscious layer of dulce de leche and rolled in coconut are perfect just the way they are.

For the Dulce de Leche

1 (14-oz [307-ml]) can condensed milk

For the Cookies

¾ cup (150 g) granulated sugar

Zest of 1 large lemon

¾ cup plus 2 tbsp (200 g) unsalted butter, room temperature

3 large egg yolks, room temperature

2 tsp (10 ml) vanilla extract

1½ cups (190 g) all-purpose flour, plus more for kneading

2 cups (255 g) cornstarch

2 tsp (9 g) baking powder

¼ tsp salt

⅓ cup (30 g) unsweetened shredded coconut, for rolling

Tips: You can use store-bought dulce de leche if you wish.

For a more intense coconut flavor, replace 1 teaspoon of vanilla extract with 1 teaspoon of coconut extract and add to the cookie dough after adding the eggs.

Make the dulce de leche first. Preheat the oven to 350°F (180°C), then pour the condensed milk into a 9-inch (23-cm) deep pie dish and cover tightly with foil. Set the plate in a roasting pan and add enough hot water into the pan to reach halfway up the sides of the pie plate. Bake in the middle of the oven for 45 minutes, and then check the water level and top up if any has evaporated. Continue to bake for another 45 to 60 minutes, or until the condensed milk is thick and golden in color (or until the depth of color is as desired). Remove the pie dish from the water bath and cool, uncovered. Whisk well to remove the lumps. This makes about 1¼ cups (300 ml). Unused dulce de leche can be stored in an airtight container and refrigerated for up to 3 weeks.

To make the cookies, in a small bowl, combine the sugar and lemon zest and using your fingertips, rub them together for 1 minute to release the oils of the zest into the sugar. In the bowl of an electric stand mixer fitted with the paddle attachment, cream the butter and sugar-zest mixture on medium speed for 5 minutes, or until pale. Reduce the speed to low and add the egg yolks and vanilla, beating until well incorporated. Scrape down the sides and bottom of the bowl.

In a separate bowl, sift the flour, cornstarch, baking powder and salt, and then stir to combine. Add the prepared flour mix to the mixing bowl and beat to combine until the dough has come together. Tip the dough onto a lightly floured countertop and knead a couple of times until smooth. Line two large baking sheets with parchment paper. Roll out the dough to a ¼-inch (6-mm) thickness, and then cut out as many rounds as you can with a 2-inch (5-cm) round cutter. If at any point the dough becomes too warm, place it into the fridge for a few minutes to chill, and then continue cutting out rounds. Re-roll the remaining scraps and repeat. Place the cookies on the baking sheet in the fridge for 30 minutes to firm up.

Bake the cookies for 8 to 10 minutes until just set and golden brown around the edges. You want the cookies to stay pale with a crumbly texture. Leave to cool completely before sandwiching two cookies together with a teaspoonful of dulce de leche in between. Once all the cookies are sandwiched together, roll them in the shredded coconut so that the coconut sticks to the dulce de leche. Alfajores can be stored in the fridge in an airtight container for up to 6 days or in the freezer for 3 to 4 weeks.

TAHINI-SWIRLED DARK CHOCOLATE BROWNIES

Yield: **16 *brownies***

We all love a good brownie. For me, rich, decadent and fudgy are my criteria for a fantastic brownie, and this recipe doesn't disappoint. I've catapulted these brownies to new levels of deliciousness by adding sesame. I've always loved sesame snaps (a sesame toffee brittle that I enjoyed snacking on when we lived in Asia) and came up with the idea of swirling sweetened tahini on the top of the brownies and crumbling sesame snaps into the batter. The sesame snaps melt during baking, which results in chewy, nutty morsels inside the brownie interior. Decadently divine!

2 cups (300 g) coarsely chopped 70% dark chocolate, divided

1 cup (230 g) unsalted butter

¾ cup (150 g) granulated sugar

¾ cup (165 g) firmly packed light brown sugar

2 large eggs plus 2 large egg yolks, room temperature and beaten

½ cup (120 ml) tahini, divided

1 tsp vanilla extract

1⅓ cups (165 g) all-purpose flour

½ cup (45 g) unsweetened cocoa powder

1 tsp salt

¾ cup (110 g) coarsely chopped sesame snaps

2 tbsp (30 ml) maple syrup

Preheat the oven to 350°F (180°C). Grease a 9 x 9–inch (23 x 23–cm) baking pan and line it with parchment paper. Allow the parchment paper to hang over the sides to make it easier to lift the brownies out once cooked.

Melt 1 cup (150 g) of the chocolate and the butter in a bowl over a pan of simmering water, ensuring the bottom of the bowl does not come into contact with the water. Stir to combine. Once melted, add the granulated sugar and light brown sugar, and stir until melted. Remove the bowl from the heat. In the bowl of an electric stand mixer fitted with the whisk attachment, add the eggs and egg yolks, ¼ cup (60 ml) of the tahini and the vanilla and whisk on medium speed until combined. Scrape the sides and bottom of the bowl. Whisking continuously, slowly pour in the melted chocolate and butter.

In a separate bowl, sift the flour, cocoa powder and salt and mix. Using a rubber spatula, gently fold the dry ingredients and the remaining chopped chocolate and sesame snaps into the chocolate batter until evenly incorporated. Pour the batter into the prepared baking pan and level with an offset spatula. In a small bowl, mix together the remaining tahini and maple syrup. Dollop the tahini mix in spoonfuls onto the brownie batter and use a toothpick to create swirls.

Bake for 25 to 30 minutes on the middle rack in the oven until the brownies are just set to touch. Don't overbake the brownies, as they will continue to set as they cool. Allow to cool in the baking pan for 10 minutes, and then, using the parchment paper, lift the brownie square out onto a wire rack and leave to cool completely before cutting into 16 pieces. Brownies can be stored at room temperature in an airtight container for up to 3 days or in the freezer for 3 months.

Tip: If you are having trouble finding sesame snaps at your local grocery store, you can buy Amki or Loucks Sezme Sesame Snaps online.

WHITE CHOCOLATE MACADAMIA NUT BLONDIES

Yield: **16** *blondies*

I was first introduced to blondies while I was living in Australia, as blondies are a big deal on their sunny shores. Ashamedly, before that I had never heard of them! Where I worked for nearly ten years as an interior designer, there was a fantastic café in a shopping center opposite us that would sell the most delicious white chocolate macadamia blondies. So, as an ode to the copious amounts that I devoured, I've created my own version that I hope you'll enjoy as much as I did for all those years!

1½ cups (230 g) coarsely chopped white chocolate, divided, plus ⅓ cup (50 g) for drizzling

¾ cup (170 g) unsalted butter

1¼ cups (275 g) firmly packed light brown sugar

2 large eggs plus 1 large egg yolk, room temperature and beaten

1 tsp vanilla extract

1¾ cups (220 g) all-purpose flour

1½ tsp (7 g) baking powder

½ tsp salt

1 cup (120 g) coarsely chopped macadamia nuts

1 tsp natural sea salt flakes (optional)

Preheat the oven to 350°F (180°C). Grease a 9 x 9–inch (23 x 23–cm) baking pan and line it with parchment paper. Allow the parchment paper to hang over the sides to make it easier to lift the blondies out once cooked.

Melt ¾ cup (115 g) of the white chocolate and the butter in a bowl set over a pan of simmering water, ensuring the bottom of the bowl does not come into contact with the water. Stir until the butter and chocolate have fully melted. Add the light brown sugar into the white chocolate, and stir until the sugar has melted. Remove from the heat and allow to cool for 10 minutes or so. Whisking the white chocolate mixture continuously, pour in the beaten eggs and vanilla.

In a separate bowl, sift the flour, baking powder and salt, and then stir to combine. Add the prepared flour mix, remaining white chocolate and macadamia nuts to the mixing bowl, and fold through until just combined. Pour the batter into the prepared baking pan and level with an offset spatula. Bake for 20 to 25 minutes, or until lightly browned on top and the sides are just set but the center is still a bit jiggly. Don't overbake the blondies, as they will continue to set as they cool. Allow to cool in the baking pan for 10 minutes, and then, using the parchment paper, lift the blondie square out onto a wire rack and leave it to cool completely before cutting into 16 pieces. Melt the ⅓ cup (50 g) of white chocolate in the microwave in 20-second increments, stirring well after each. Drizzle the melted chocolate over the blondies and sprinkle with flaked sea salt, if using.

These blondies can be stored at room temperature in an airtight container for up to 3 days or in the freezer for 3 months.

Tip: The flaked sea salt cuts through the sweetness of the blondies. Essential in my opinion, but ultimately, this extra salt is optional.

ESPRESSO MILLIONAIRE SHORTBREAD BARS

Yield: **16 bars**

What's not to love about a layer of buttery, crumbly shortbread slathered with oozing caramel and topped with decadent chocolate? These bars are a delicious British classic at heart. Here I've included espresso powder in the caramel layer which, despite being only a one-ingredient addition, totally transforms these millionaire bars.

For the Shortbread

1²/₃ cups (210 g) all-purpose flour

²/₃ cup (150 g) unsalted butter, room temperature

¹/₃ cup (65 g) granulated sugar

1 large egg yolk

1 tsp vanilla extract

¹/₂ tsp salt

For the Espresso Caramel

2 (14-oz [307-ml]) cans condensed milk

1 cup (230 g) unsalted butter

¹/₂ cup (110 g) firmly packed light brown sugar

¹/₂ cup (120 ml) golden syrup

2 tsp (4 g) espresso powder

¹/₂ tsp salt

For the Chocolate Layer

1²/₃ cups (250 g) coarsely chopped 70% dark chocolate

2 tbsp (30 g) unsalted butter

¹/₃ cup (50 g) chopped white chocolate, for feathering

Tip: This makes an extra-thick layer of caramel. If you prefer a thinner layer, halve the caramel ingredients.

Preheat the oven to 350°F (180°C). Grease a 9 x 9–inch (23 x 23–cm) baking pan and line with parchment paper. Allow the parchment paper to hang over the sides to make it easier to lift the shortbread out once cooked.

To make the shortbread base, in the bowl of a stand mixer fitted with a paddle attachment, add the flour, butter, sugar, egg yolk, vanilla and salt and beat on medium speed until combined and a dough starts to form. Tip the dough into the prepared pan and using your hands, press the mixture into the pan until totally level. Using the base of a measuring cup or glass might help to level at the end. Prick the base all over with the tines of a fork. Bake for 20 to 25 minutes, or until golden. Remove the pan from the oven and allow it to cool completely.

To make the caramel layer, in a medium saucepan over low heat, add the condensed milk, butter, brown sugar, golden syrup, espresso powder and salt and heat until the sugar has dissolved and the butter has melted, about 5 minutes. Increase the heat, and bring the mixture to a boil, stirring continuously so that it doesn't catch. The caramel will thicken to a soft fudge consistency and turn golden brown. This can take about 5 minutes. Pour the caramel onto the cooled shortbread base, level with an offset spatula and leave to set for 1 hour in the fridge.

To make the feathered chocolate layer, melt the dark chocolate and butter in a bowl set over a pan of simmering water, ensuring the bottom of the bowl does not come into contact with the water. Once melted and glossy, pour the chocolate mixture over the caramel. Melt the white chocolate in the microwave in 20-second increments, stirring well after each.

Spoon melted white chocolate into a small piping bag and pipe horizontal straight lines about ¼ inch (6 mm) apart over the dark chocolate. Score the lines using a skewer by dragging it up and down the top of the chocolate, perpendicular to the lines that you piped. Chill in the fridge until completely set, at least 1 hour or overnight. Remove from the pan by using the parchment paper. Cut into slices or squares using a sharp, hot knife, wiping between each cut. These shortbread bars can be stored at room temperature in an airtight container for up to 1 week.

TAKE-ME-BACK WAGON WHEEL SLICE

Yield: **16** *slices*

This famous snack graced the lunch boxes of millions of school children, and I for one LOVED them as a kid. I hadn't eaten one in 20 years before recipe testing (I know, shock, horror), but one bite and I was taken back to my weekly trips to the school tuck shop. This is a super-fun version that I hope will become a family favorite. Layers of crunchy shortbread, raspberry jam, legendary marshmallow and chocolate coating create this sticky delight. Perfect for a birthday party, backyard barbeque or movie night at home.

For the Shortbread

1⅔ cups (210 g) all-purpose flour

⅔ cup (150 g) unsalted butter, room temperature, cut into small cubes

⅓ cup (65 g) granulated sugar

1 large egg yolk

1 tsp vanilla extract

½ tsp salt

1 cup (320 g) raspberry jam

For the Marshmallow

⅔ cup (160 ml) water, divided

1½ tsp (5 g) gelatin powder

1 cup (200 g) granulated sugar

⅛ cup (30 ml) liquid glucose syrup

¼ tsp salt

1 large egg white

1 tsp vanilla bean paste

Preheat the oven to 350°F (180°C). Grease a 9 x 9–inch (23 x 23–cm) baking pan and line it with parchment paper. Allow the parchment paper to hang over the sides to make it easier to lift the slice out once cooked.

To make the shortbread base, in the bowl of a stand mixer fitted with a paddle attachment, add the flour, butter, sugar, egg yolk, vanilla and salt, and beat on medium speed until combined and a dough starts to form. Add the dough into the prepared pan, and using your hands, press the mixture into the pan until totally level. Using the base of a measuring cup or glass might help to level at the end. Prick the base all over with the tines of a fork. Bake for 20 to 25 minutes, or until golden. Remove from the oven and spread the jam over the warm base. Allow to cool completely.

To make the marshmallow layer, place ⅓ cup (80 ml) of the water in a bowl. Add the gelatin powder and mix to moisten the gelatin. Set aside for at least 10 minutes to allow the gelatin to bloom while the sugar syrup is cooking. In a pan, add the sugar, glucose, salt and remaining water, and cook over low heat to dissolve. Increase to medium heat and bring to a boil. Cook until the syrup reaches soft-ball 244°F (118°C) on a candy thermometer. Then add the gelatin, whisking all the time. Be careful as it will bubble up. Whisk until the gelatin dissolves, and then remove from the heat and set aside.

(continued)

For the Chocolate Layer

1 cup (150 g) coarsely chopped 70% dark chocolate

⅔ cup (100 g) coarsely chopped milk chocolate

2 tbsp (30 g) butter

While the syrup is cooking, add the egg white to the bowl of a stand mixer fitted with a whisk attachment and whisk on medium-high speed until soft peaks form, about 5 minutes. Turn the mixer to low speed, and then pour in the sugar syrup in a steady stream down the side of the stand mixer bowl (not onto the whisk blades). Add the vanilla bean paste and gradually increase the speed of the mixer until it's running on high. Whip the marshmallow mixture for 10 minutes, or until it has tripled in size and is stiff and shiny. Spoon the marshmallow over the jam layer and quickly level it out with an oiled offset spatula. Allow to cool completely.

While the marshmallow is cooling, make the chocolate layer. Melt the dark and milk chocolate and butter in a bowl set over a pan of simmering water, ensuring the bottom of the bowl does not come into contact with the water. Once melted and glossy, remove the bowl from the heat, set aside for 10 minutes and allow to cool slightly. Pour it over the marshmallow layer and smooth out with an offset spatula. Refrigerate for 2 hours or until the chocolate has set.

Let stand at room temperature for 10 minutes before slicing into 16 squares. Note the chocolate can tend to crack. What I found worked best was to heat my knife blade in the flames of the gas stovetop, or run the knife under boiling water and carefully dry. Then, where I wanted to cut, I just placed the blade onto the chocolate, and with gentle pressure let the heat melt the chocolate down to the marshmallow layer. Then I cut through. Each time I make a cut, I wash, dry and reheat the blade. This does take time to get these clean cuts, so it depends on whether you have the patience! This slice can be stored in the fridge in an airtight container for up to 4 days.

Tip: You can also use store-bought marshmallows. Cut the marshmallows in half and place the cut side down over the jam layer. In a 350°F (180°C) preheated oven, bake for 2 to 6 minutes until the marshmallows are melted. Remove from the oven. Using an offset spatula, smooth the surface of the marshmallows to create a level surface. Cool in the pan before carrying on with the melted chocolate layer.

PASSION FRUIT VANILLA SLICE

Yield: **12–16** *slices*

Custard slice, vanilla slice, *mille-feuille*, Napoleon . . . whatever you'd like to call it, it's hard to deny that this is a pastry classic. I adore anything custard-based, so it goes without saying that I love the crunchy puff pastry sandwiching the smooth, rich custard layer. In Australia, I grew to love tropical passion fruit, and it lends itself so well to this elegant dessert. In my recipe, I share a super-simple way to ensure you cut through the pastry and custard to give yourself beautiful slices.

For the Puff Pastry
2 sheets puff pastry, partially thawed

For the Passion Fruit Custard
4 cups (960 ml) whole milk

1 cup (200 g) granulated sugar, divided

7 egg yolks, room temperature

½ cup plus 2 tsp (70 g) cornstarch

½ tsp salt

Pulp of 6 passion fruits

½ cup (115 g) unsalted butter, room temperature

1 tsp vanilla bean paste

Preheat the oven to 350°F (180°C), and line two baking sheets with parchment paper.

To prepare the pastry, place 1 sheet of pastry on each tray and prick all over with a fork. Place another piece of parchment paper on top of each pastry sheet. Add another baking sheet on top as this will ensure that the pastry won't rise too much. Bake for 30 minutes, or until the pastry is golden and crispy, rotating the pans halfway through. Remove the top pan and the parchment paper and set the pastry aside to cool completely.

Grease a 9 x 9–inch (23 x 23–cm) baking pan and line with parchment paper. Allow the parchment paper to hang over the sides to make it easier to lift the slice out once cooked. Using a sharp knife, cut each pastry sheet into a 9-inch (23-cm) square, trimming as needed. You now have your top and bottom pastry layers. Place 1 piece of pastry in the prepared pan to form the bottom layer.

To make the custard, in a saucepan over medium heat, heat the milk and ½ cup (100 g) of the sugar until just simmering and bubbles appear around the edge, but not boiling. Remove from the heat. In a large bowl placed on a tea towel (to prevent it from slipping), add the remaining sugar, egg yolks, cornstarch and salt, and whisk until pale and combined. While continuously whisking the egg mixture, slowly pour in one-quarter of the milk mixture in a thin steady stream to temper it. Then gradually add the remaining milk mixture, whisking until well combined. Pour the mixture back into the saucepan and scoop the passion fruit pulp into the custard. Cook the custard on medium-low heat while whisking constantly, until it starts to thicken. Ensure that it doesn't boil, otherwise the custard will curdle. Turn the heat down to low and keep whisking for 2 minutes until you have a smooth custard that thickly coats the back of a wooden spoon. Strain the custard through a sieve set over a medium bowl, discarding the passion fruit seeds. Add the butter and vanilla bean paste and whisk until melted. Allow to cool for 10 minutes, and then pour the custard over the bottom layer of pastry in the prepared pan, and with an offset spatula, smooth it out evenly right up to the edges.

(continued)

For the Passion Fruit Icing

1 cup (120 g) confectioners' sugar

1 passion fruit

1 tbsp (15 ml) milk, plus more as needed

Notes: This slice can be cut into smaller squares by cutting the top pastry layer into 16 squares.

If passion fruit is not in season or readily available at your local grocery store, then a good substitute is canned passion fruit pulp, which you can order online.

If you only have two baking sheets, you can bake one pastry at a time.

To make this into a vanilla slice, omit the passion fruit from the custard and icing and replace in the glaze with 1 teaspoon of vanilla extract.

Cut the remaining piece of pastry into 12 even rectangles. Precutting the top layer of pastry now makes it easier to cut neat slices later on. A super-simple but effective trick! Gently place the cut-out pastry squares on top of the custard layer, laying them right up next to each other to form the top pastry layer of the slice. With a pen, mark on the parchment paper where the precut joins of the pastry are. When the icing covers the pastry, it becomes hard to see the joins of the pastry, and the marked lines help guide you on where to cut. Chill for at least 6 hours (ideally overnight) until set.

To make the passion fruit icing, use a fine-mesh sieve to sift the confectioners' sugar into a medium mixing bowl. Scoop the pulp and seeds from the passion fruit and add them to the bowl along with the milk. Whisk until you have a smooth, thick glaze. If the glaze is too thick, add more milk, 1 teaspoon at a time, until you've reached your desired consistency. I prefer the icing to be on the thicker side so it holds its shape when the slices are cut.

Pour the passion fruit icing over the slice, and level using the back of a spoon. Allow the icing to set for 1 hour in the fridge. Then, using the parchment paper, gently lift the slice out of the pan onto a chopping board, and using a sharp knife, slice into 12 squares following the precut pastry squares as a guide. This slice is best served immediately but can be stored in the fridge in an airtight container for up to 3 days.

COMFORTING PIES AND TARTS

Pies and tarts embody home comforts, don't they!? That flaky pastry, sweet filling . . . it's an emotional blanket of familiarity and love that just wraps itself around you. Making pies and, in particular, tarts has to be one of my favorite things to do. From the variety of pastries that you can create to the multitude of fillings that you can tuck inside, they will always be enjoyed.

In this chapter, I've included various pastry doughs for you to try out, from sour cream shortcrust pastry (pages 39 and 41) made in the food processor to our all-butter shortcrust pastry (page 48 and 65) and sweet shortcrust pastry (pages 45, 51 and 60) made by hand. With lots of step-by-step images taking you through the stages of making pastry, my hope is for you to enjoy making it as much as I do.

You'll find plenty of fruit-filled tarts given that fruit lends itself so beautifully to being baked with pastry. The Dark Chocolate Cherry Galette (page 45), the French beauty Lemon Pistachio Tart (page 51) and the Italian classic Mixed Berry Lattice Crostata (page 54) will be sure to please a crowd.

For an understated pie, I love The Ultimate Chocolate Banoffee Pie (page 69) with its chocolate biscuit base, gooey chocolate caramel filling, freshly sliced bananas and mounds of whipped cream. It's a British classic that needs to be shared globally!

BLUEBERRY LEMON THYME PIE WITH SOUR CREAM PASTRY

Yield: 1 *(9-inch [23-cm]) pie (10-12 slices)*

A homemade fruit-filled pie is as heartwarming as visiting your grandma's house as a child, sitting on her lap and cuddling up while reading your favorite book. It just has that effect on you! While most find the classic apple pie to be truly nostalgic, my blueberry pie combines the familiarity of fresh blueberries alongside zesty lemon and fragrant thyme, encased in flaky sour cream shortcrust pastry, for a flavor-packed pie that will have you making new and delicious memories.

For the Sour Cream Shortcrust Pastry

2 tbsp (30 g) granulated sugar

Zest of 1 large lemon

3 cups (375 g) all-purpose flour

½ tsp salt

2 tbsp (4 g) fresh thyme leaves

1 cup (230 g) cold unsalted butter, chopped into small cubes

½ cup plus 2 tbsp (150 ml) sour cream, plus extra if needed

For the Blueberry Filling

½ cup (100 g) granulated sugar

3 tbsp (25 g) cornstarch

Zest of 1 large lemon

4⅔ cups (700 g) ripe blueberries, rinsed and dried

1 small apple, peeled, cored and grated

2 tbsp (30 ml) golden syrup

2 tbsp (30 ml) fresh lemon juice

1 tbsp (2 g) fresh thyme leaves

To make the sour cream shortcrust pastry, in a small bowl, combine the sugar and lemon zest, and using your fingertips, rub the two together for 1 minute to release the oils of the zest into the sugar. Place the sugar-zest mixture, flour, salt and thyme leaves into the canister of a food processor. Pulse briefly to mix. Add the cubed butter and pulse until the mixture resembles coarse breadcrumbs with some pea-sized butter pieces still visible. It should take two or three pulses. Add the sour cream and pulse again until the mixture begins to clump together. If the dough isn't coming together in the first few pulses, add more sour cream, 1 teaspoon at a time. Turn the dough out onto a lightly floured countertop. Use floured hands to shape the dough into a ball, taking care not to overwork it. Split the ball in half and flatten slightly into two discs. Wrap each disc well with plastic wrap and place into the fridge for at least 1 hour to let the dough rest.

To make the blueberry filling, in a large bowl, whisk together the sugar, cornstarch and lemon zest. Add the blueberries, apple, golden syrup, lemon juice and thyme leaves. Use a large spoon to gently toss and coat the blueberries. Set aside until the berries start to release their juices, about 20 minutes.

Preheat the oven to 425°F (220°C). Flour the base of a 9-inch (23-cm) deep pie pan. Remove the chilled dough discs from the fridge and set them aside for 5 to 10 minutes—this allows the dough to warm up slightly so the edges don't crack. With the first disc, lightly flour your countertop and rolling pin, and using firm, even strokes, roll from the center outward, turning the dough a quarter turn every few strokes. Roll the dough out to the thickness of a coin (⅛ inch [3 mm] thick) and into a 12-inch (30-cm) circle. Gently lift the dough and place into the prepared dish. Trim the edges to within ¼ inch (6 mm) of the dish edge. Spoon the blueberry filling into the pie base in the prepared dish, leaving behind any excess liquid.

Prepare the pie top by rolling the second disc of dough out to the thickness of a coin (⅛ inch [3 mm] thick) and into a 12-inch (30-cm) circle. Gently place it on top of the blueberry filling. Trim the edges with a sharp knife. With the tines of a fork, firmly press down on the edges to crimp and seal them.

(continued)

For the Topping
1 small egg
1 tbsp (15 ml) milk
1 tbsp (15 g) coarse turbinado sugar

Tips: Refer to the Apricot Almond Bakewell Tart recipe on page 42 for images of making sour cream shortcrust pastry in a food processor.

For a simpler look, you can crimp the edges of the crust with your fingers. Brush on the egg wash and sprinkle with sugar as normal.

For the topping, form the excess dough into a ball and roll out to ⅛ inch (3 mm) thick. Using a leaf pastry cutter or cutter of your choice, stamp out enough shapes to go around the edge. Make an egg wash by whisking together the egg and milk in a small bowl. Brush the edges of the pie with egg wash and place the leaf cutouts around in an overlapping pattern. Brush the top of the pie and leaves with egg wash. Score the top of the dough with four cuts in the center to create steam vents. Sprinkle with the turbinado sugar.

Place the pie onto a large baking sheet and bake for 20 minutes. Reduce the heat to 350°F (180°C) and bake for 30 to 40 minutes, or until juices are bubbling and have thickened. When you reduce the heat of the oven, cover the edge of the pie with foil or a pie crust shield to prevent the edges from browning too much. Transfer to a wire rack to cool completely before serving. This blueberry pie can be stored, covered loosely in plastic wrap at room temperature, for up to 2 days or in the fridge for up to 4 to 5 days.

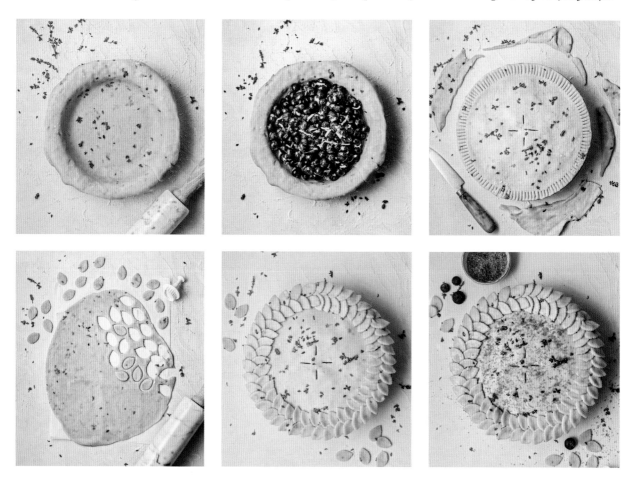

APRICOT ALMOND BAKEWELL TART

Yield: 1 *(9-inch [23-cm]) tart (10-12 slices)*

My grandparents lived in the beautiful spa town of Buxton in Derbyshire, Northern England, and when we'd make the two-and-a-half hour drive up to visit them, we'd often stop off to stretch our legs and have a tea break. I distinctly remember stopping off one time in the market town of Bakewell and being introduced to the Bakewell tart, which the town is famous for. I was bowled over with how delicious the combination of shortcrust pastry, jam and frangipane filling was in a tart. My version is an ode to summer, with lemon in the filling and icing and the seasonal apricot within. Just thinking of this tart makes me smile.

For the Sour Cream Shortcrust Pastry

1½ cups (190 g) all-purpose flour

1 tbsp (15 g) granulated sugar

¼ tsp salt

½ cup (115 g) cold unsalted butter, chopped into small cubes

¼ cup plus 1 tbsp (75 ml) sour cream, plus extra if needed

1 small egg

1 tbsp (15 ml) milk

¾ cup (240 g) apricot jam

5 apricots (about 250 g), halved and destoned

For the Frangipane Filling

½ cup (115 g) unsalted butter, room temperature

½ cup (100 g) granulated sugar

Zest of 1 large lemon

2 large eggs, room temperature

1 cup (100 g) almond meal

⅔ cup (85 g) all-purpose flour

1 tsp vanilla extract

1 tsp almond extract

¼ tsp salt

To make the sour cream shortcrust pastry, add the flour, sugar and salt into the canister of a food processor. Pulse briefly to mix. Add the cubed butter and pulse until the mixture resembles coarse breadcrumbs with some pea-sized butter pieces still visible. It should take two or three pulses. Add the sour cream and pulse again until the mixture begins to clump together. If the dough isn't coming together after the first few pulses, add more sour cream, 1 teaspoon at a time. Carefully remove the blade of the food processor and then turn out the dough onto a lightly floured countertop. Use floured hands to shape the dough into a ball, taking care not to overwork it. Flatten slightly into a disc and wrap well in plastic wrap. Place in the fridge for at least 1 hour to let the dough rest.

Remove the chilled dough disc from the fridge and set it aside on your countertop for 5 to 10 minutes to allow the dough to warm up slightly so it's easier to roll out. Trying to roll dough that is too cold will cause the edges to crack. To roll out, lightly flour your countertop and rolling pin, and using firm, even strokes, roll from the center outward, turning the dough a quarter turn every few strokes. Roll the dough out to the thickness of a coin (⅛ inch [3 mm] thick) and into a 12-inch (30-cm) circle. Flour the base of a 9-inch (23-cm) deep fluted tart pan with removable base, and gently lift the dough and place into the prepared pan. Use your fingers to push the dough up the sides of the pan. Using a sharp knife, trim off the excess dough from the rim. Refrigerate the prepared tart shell for at least 30 minutes to allow the dough to relax further. My preference is to leave the shell overnight in the fridge and continue with the recipe the next day. If you do this, make sure to cover well in plastic wrap to ensure the dough doesn't dry out.

Preheat the oven to 350°F (180°C).

(continued)

For the Lemon Icing

1½ cups (180 g) confectioners' sugar

2 tbsp (30 ml) lemon juice, plus more if needed

2 tbsp (15 g) toasted slivered almonds

Notes: Traditional Bakewell tarts include the icing layer, but if this will be too sweet for you, omit the icing and simply dust with 1 teaspoon of confectioners' sugar and top with the almonds.

Prick the tart base all over with a fork, and then line with parchment paper and fill with pie weights all the way up the sides. Blind bake for 15 minutes, and then remove the parchment paper and pie weights. Make an egg wash by whisking together the egg and milk in a small bowl. Brush the base of the tart shell with egg wash and return the base back to the oven and bake for 7 to 10 minutes, or until the base is dry and a light golden color. Remove from the oven and leave to cool. Spread the apricot jam over the base of the tart shell to form a thick layer. Cut each apricot half into four if the apricots are small, or cut each half into eight if the apricots are large. Lay the apricot slices over the jam layer.

To make the frangipane filling, in the bowl of an electric stand mixer fitted with the paddle attachment, beat the butter, sugar and lemon zest together on medium speed for 5 minutes, or until pale. Add the eggs one at a time, beating between each addition, scraping down the sides of the bowl every so often. Add the almond meal, flour, vanilla, almond extract and salt and mix until combined. Dollop the frangipane filling over the jam and apricot slices. Using the back of the spoon, gently spread the filling to evenly cover the apricots, and ensure that it sits ¼ inch (6 mm) or so from the top of the tart shell. The filling will puff up, and you need a lip for the glaze to run into once baked. Place the tart pan onto a baking sheet. Bake for 35 to 45 minutes, or until the pastry is golden and the filling is just firm to the touch. Leave to cool in the pan for 10 minutes, and then lift the tart onto a wire rack and leave to cool completely.

To make the lemon icing, use a fine-mesh sieve to sift the confectioners' sugar into a medium mixing bowl. Whisk in the lemon juice until you have a smooth, thick glaze. If the glaze is too thick, add more lemon juice, 1 teaspoon at a time, until you've reached your desired consistency. Spread the icing over the top of the cold tart and sprinkle with slivered almonds. Let it stand for 20 minutes, or until the icing has set before you slice. This tart can be stored at room temperature wrapped in plastic wrap for up to 2 days or in the fridge for up to 4 days.

DARK CHOCOLATE CHERRY GALETTE

Yield: 1 *(8–9-inch [20–23-cm]) galette (8–10 slices)*

Galettes have to be one of the simplest "pies" that you can make, as they taste exactly like pie but without all the fuss. Because a galette is a free-form tart, you really can't go wrong, as you can shape it as rustically as you like. The filling options are endless, but one of my favorites to use is cherries. This tiny stone fruit is one of summer's true jewels. I adore them, especially with dark chocolate. In this galette, the sweet, flaky pastry is layered with the cheeky addition of melted dark chocolate and then the sweet juicy cherries atop. One bite and I'm transported to San Diego on my family holiday, enjoying a slice of all-American cherry pie.

For the Sweet Shortcrust Pastry

1¾ cups (220 g) all-purpose flour

⅓ cup (40 g) confectioners' sugar

½ tsp salt

½ cup (115 g) cold unsalted butter, chopped into small cubes

1 large egg, cold and beaten

1–2 tbsp (15–30 ml) ice-cold water

For the Cherry Filling and Toppings

4 cups (600 g) fresh pitted cherries

⅓ cup (70 g) firmly packed brown sugar

2 tbsp (15 g) cornstarch

2 tsp (10 ml) fresh lemon juice

1 tsp almond extract

¼ tsp of salt

To make the sweet shortcrust pastry, in a large mixing bowl, sift the flour, confectioners' sugar and salt. Add the butter and toss until the cubes are coated. Rub the mixture together between your fingers until it reaches a breadcrumb consistency with some hazelnut-sized butter pieces still visible. Make a well in the center of the flour and add the egg. Using a fork, mix the egg into the flour. Add 1 tablespoon (15 ml) of the ice-cold water and use your fingertips to bring the dough together. If the dough isn't clumping together, add more water sparingly. Tip the dough onto a lightly floured countertop and use floured hands to shape dough into a ball, taking care not to overwork it. Flatten slightly into a disc and wrap well in plastic wrap. Place in the fridge for at least 1 hour to let the dough rest.

To prepare the cherry filling, slice two-thirds of the cherries in half, leaving the remainder whole. In a large bowl, add the brown sugar and cornstarch and mix. Add all the sliced and whole cherries, lemon juice, almond extract and salt. Toss well to coat the cherries and set aside to macerate for 20 minutes while your dough comes to room temperature in the next step.

(continued)

⅔ cup (100 g) finely chopped 70% dark chocolate

1 small egg

1 tbsp (15 ml) milk

¼ cup (30 g) slivered almonds

1 tbsp (15 g) coarse turbinado sugar

Vanilla bean ice cream, for serving (optional)

Line a baking sheet with parchment paper.

Remove the chilled dough disc from the fridge and set it aside on your countertop for 5 to 10 minutes to allow the dough to warm up slightly so it's easier to roll out. Trying to roll out dough that is too cold will cause the edges to crack. To roll out, lightly flour your countertop and rolling pin, and using firm, even strokes, roll from the center outward, turning the dough a quarter turn every few strokes. Roll the dough out to the thickness of a coin (⅛ inch [3 mm] thick) and into a 12-inch (30-cm) circle. Trim the rim of the circle to make a clean cut if desired or leave as is for a rustic look. Transfer the dough to the prepared baking sheet.

Preheat the oven to 375°F (190°C) and set a rack in the center of the oven.

Sprinkle the chopped chocolate over the base of the dough, leaving a 2-inch (5-cm) border all around. Spoon the cherries (not the juice so as to prevent the dough from becoming soggy) onto the chocolate circle. Gently fold the edges of the dough inward, working around the cherries, pleating the dough as you work your way around. Press gently to seal the folds. Cover the galette with plastic wrap and rest in the fridge for at least 20 minutes. Make an egg wash by whisking together the egg and milk in a small bowl. Brush the crust with the egg wash. Sprinkle almonds and turbinado sugar around the galette rim.

Bake the galette for 40 to 45 minutes, rotating once while baking. The pastry should be golden and crisp when ready. Allow to sit for 10 minutes before serving. Serve with vanilla bean ice cream for the tastiest experience. This galette is best eaten immediately but can be kept wrapped loosely in plastic wrap at room temperature for up to 2 days.

FESTIVE CRANBERRY LEMON MERINGUE PIE

Yield: 1 *(9-inch [23-cm]) pie (10-12 slices)*

The perfect pie for Thanksgiving or Christmas, this pie uses seasonal cranberries in its cranberry lemon curd filling to add another layer of interest. Topped with swaths of pillowy meringue, this is a showstopper that will enthrall those who bite into this texturally beautiful pie. Fondly remember holidays gone by—or make some new, festive memories—as you bite into this delicious masterpiece!

For the All-Butter Shortcrust Pastry

1¾ cups (220 g) all-purpose flour

¼ tsp salt

½ cup plus 1 tbsp (130 g) cold unsalted butter, chopped into small cubes

3-4 tbsp (45-60 ml) water, plus more if needed

1 small egg

1 tbsp (15 ml) milk

To make the all-butter shortcrust pastry, into a large mixing bowl, sift in the flour and salt. Add the butter and toss until the cubes are coated. Rub the mixture together between your fingers until it reaches a breadcrumb consistency with a few walnut half–sized pieces of butter still visible. Add the water, and use your fingertips to bring the dough together. If the dough isn't clumping together, add more water sparingly. Tip the dough onto a lightly floured countertop and use floured hands to shape the dough into a ball, taking care not to overwork it. Flatten the dough slightly into a disc, and wrap well in plastic wrap. Place in the fridge for at least 1 hour to let the dough rest.

Remove the chilled dough disc from the fridge and set it aside on your countertop for 5 to 10 minutes to allow the dough to warm up slightly so it's easier to roll out. Trying to roll dough that is too cold will cause the edges to crack. To roll out, lightly flour your countertop and rolling pin, and using firm, even strokes, roll from the center outward, turning the dough a quarter turn every few strokes. Roll the dough out to the thickness of a coin (⅛ inch [3 mm] thick) and into a 12-inch (30-cm) circle. Flour the base of a 9-inch (23-cm) shallow fluted tart pan with a removable base, and gently lift the dough and place into the prepared pan. Use your fingers to push the dough up the sides of the pan and into the grooves. Using a sharp knife, trim off the excess dough from the rim. Refrigerate the prepared tart shell for at least 1 hour to allow the dough to relax further. My preference is to leave the shell overnight in the fridge and continue with the recipe the next day. If you do this, cover well in plastic wrap to ensure that the dough doesn't dry out.

Preheat the oven to 350°F (180°C).

Once the dough is chilled, prick the tart base all over with a fork, and then line with parchment paper and fill with pie weights all the way up the sides. Blind bake for 15 minutes, and then remove the parchment paper and pie weights. Make an egg wash by whisking together the egg and milk in a small bowl. Brush the base of the tart shell with the egg wash, and return it to the oven and bake for 7 to 10 minutes, or until the base is dry and a light golden color. The tart base can be made the day before.

(continued)

For the Cranberry Lemon Curd Filling

4 cups (400 g) fresh or frozen cranberries

Zest of 4 large lemons

3 tbsp (45 ml) water

1 cup (200 g) granulated sugar

¼ cup (30 g) cornstarch

¾ cup (180 ml) fresh lemon juice (about 4 lemons)

½ cup (115 g) unsalted butter, cut into small pieces

4 large egg yolks plus 1 whole large egg

⅓ cup (80 ml) heavy cream

For the Meringue

6 large egg whites

1½ cups (300 g) superfine caster sugar

2 tsp (5 g) cornstarch

1 tsp fresh lemon juice

Notes: I have only tested the cranberry filling with frozen cranberries, as that was all that was available at the time. My lovely recipe tester made this with fresh cranberries and found the filling to be a little runny. I suggest adding an extra 1 tablespoon (8 g) of cornstarch to the filling if using fresh cranberries.

Refer to Chocolate Pecan Pie on page 67 for step-by-step images of making all-butter shortcrust pastry by hand.

To make the filling, combine the cranberries, lemon zest and water in a large pan over medium heat. Cover and bring to a boil, and then simmer for 10 to 15 minutes, stirring occasionally. Once the cranberries have softened, mash them with a fork. Remove from the heat and strain the cranberries through a fine-mesh sieve, discarding the solids. (You'll get approximately 1 cup (240 ml) worth of cranberry liquid.) Stir in the sugar.

In a clean saucepan, whisk the cornstarch with the lemon juice. Add the strained cranberry mixture and cook over a medium-low heat for 10 minutes, stirring constantly, until thickened. Remove from the heat and whisk in the butter until melted. Add the egg yolks one at a time, whisking well after each addition. Whisk in the whole egg and heavy cream until combined, and then return the mixture to the heat for 5 to 10 minutes, stirring until thickened. Remove from the heat and leave to cool fully. Refrigerate for 30 minutes to 1 hour. The filling can be made the day before and kept in the fridge until needed.

To make the meringue, place the egg whites in the bowl of a stand mixer fitted with the whisk attachment, and whisk on medium speed until soft peaks form when the whisk is removed, approximately 5 minutes. As you whisk, gradually add the sugar one spoonful at a time, whisking well between each spoonful. Once all the sugar is added, whisk in the cornstarch and lemon juice, and whisk for 5 minutes. By now the mixture should be thick and glossy and the sugar should be fully incorporated. If you rub a bit of mixture between your thumb and finger, there should be no grit, as the sugar should be fully blended. If there is still some grit, continue whipping for a couple more minutes.

Give the cranberry filling a quick stir to loosen. Pour the filling into the tart shell and level with the back of a spoon. Dollop meringue onto the cranberry filling and swirl the top. There is enough meringue to make a nice, high dome. Bake for 18 to 20 minutes, or until the meringue is crisp and lightly golden. Remove from the oven and leave to cool in the tart pan for 30 minutes before removing the base. Leave it to sit for another 30 minutes or so until the filling has set again. Slice and serve. This pie can be stored in an airtight container in the fridge for up to 3 days, but the meringue may start to weep.

LEMON PISTACHIO TART

Yield: 1 *(9-inch [23-cm]) tart (10-12 slices)*

This tart is my husband's personal favorite. He's held a soft spot for it in the near 20 years that I've known him. I can't blame him, as a simple French lemon tart, when done well, excels in its tangy lemony simplicity. Using classic sweet shortcrust pasty, I've added pistachios for a nutty kick and nuts on the top for extra crunch.

For the Sweet Shortcrust Pastry

⅓ cup (35 g) shelled unsalted pistachios

1¾ cups (220 g) all-purpose flour

⅓ cup (40 g) confectioners' sugar

¼ tsp salt

½ cup (115 g) cold unsalted butter, chopped into small cubes

1 large egg, cold and beaten

1–2 tsp (5–10 ml) ice-cold water, if needed

To make the sweet shortcrust pastry, crush the pistachios with a pestle and mortar until finely ground. Sift the flour, confectioners' sugar and salt into a large bowl and add the pistachios. Add the butter and toss until the cubes are coated. Rub the nuts, butter and flour together between your fingers until it reaches a breadcrumb consistency with a few hazelnut-sized pieces of butter still visible. Make a well in the center of the flour and add the egg. Using a fork, mix the egg into the flour. Using your fingertips, bring the dough together. If necessary, add 1 teaspoon of the ice-cold water, but only add the water if required, as I find the oils of the pistachio nuts provide enough moisture to the dough. Tip the dough onto a lightly floured countertop, and use floured hands to shape the dough into a ball, taking care not to overwork it. Flatten slightly into a disc, and wrap well in plastic wrap. Place in the fridge for at least 1 hour to allow the dough to rest.

Remove the chilled dough disc from the fridge and set it aside on your countertop for 5 to 10 minutes to allow the dough to warm up slightly so it's easier to roll out. Trying to roll out dough that is too cold will cause the edges to crack. To roll out, lightly flour your countertop and rolling pin, and using firm, even strokes, roll from the center outward, turning the dough a quarter turn every few strokes. Roll the dough out to the thickness of a coin (⅛ inch [3 mm] thick) and into a 12-inch (30-cm) circle. Flour the base of a 9-inch (23-cm) shallow fluted tart pan with a removable base, and gently lift the dough and place into the prepared pan. Use your fingers to push the dough up the sides of the pan and into the grooves. Using a sharp knife, trim off the excess dough from the rim. Refrigerate the prepared tart shell for at least 1 hour to allow the dough to relax further. My preference is to leave the shell in the fridge overnight and continue with the recipe the next day. If you do this, make sure to cover well in plastic wrap to ensure that the dough doesn't dry out.

(continued)

For the Lemon Tart Filling

4 large eggs, room temperature

1 cup (200 g) granulated sugar

Zest of 3 large lemons

⅓ cup plus 2 tsp (90 ml) fresh lemon juice

½ cup (120 ml) heavy cream

For the Topping

1 tbsp (8 g) confectioners' sugar, for dusting

2 tbsp (15 g) coarsely chopped toasted unsalted pistachios

Preheat the oven to 350°F (180°C).

Once the dough is chilled, prick the tart base all over with a fork, and then line with parchment paper and fill with pie weights all the way up the sides. Blind bake for 15 minutes, and then remove the parchment paper and pie weights. Return the tart shell back to the oven and bake for 15 minutes, or until the base is dry and a light golden color. Remove from the oven and leave the tart shell to cool.

To make the lemon filling, into a large mixing bowl, break the eggs and whisk together. Add the sugar, lemon zest, lemon juice and cream, and whisk again until they are all well combined. Pour the filling mixture into a pitcher or measuring cup. Skim off any bubbles from the top of the lemon cream and discard. Place the tart shell pan onto a baking sheet, as this makes it easier to transfer to the oven. Pour half of the lemon cream into the tart shell, and then transfer the shell on the baking sheet to the oven before adding the rest of the filling. (This prevents any spillage and gives a neat finish.)

Bake for 30 to 35 minutes, or until just set but with a slight wobble in the center. Leave to cool slightly, and when the filling seems firm enough, remove the tart from the pan. Transfer the tart to a serving plate, and dust with sifted confectioners' sugar. Sprinkle with chopped toasted pistachios only when ready to serve as they will soften with the moisture of the filling and lose their crunch. This lemon tart can be kept in an airtight container in the fridge for up to 2 days.

Tip: Refer to Dark Chocolate Cherry Galette on page 47 for step-by-step images of making sweet shortcrust pastry by hand.

MIXED BERRY LATTICE CROSTATA

Yield: 1 (14 x 4 ½-inch [35 x 11-cm]) rectangular tart pan (10–12 slices)

From a distance, this looks like a standard fruit lattice tart, but let me tell you . . . it's not. An Italian classic, crostata uses pasta frolla as the pastry. Traditionally tricky to roll out but incredibly easy to press into your tart pan, this orange-fragranced pastry literally melts in your mouth when eaten. Crostata is always filled with some type of jam, and here I've combined my favorite summer berries. The resulting mixed berry jam fills this beautiful tart to the brim with gorgeous flavor. I hope that you love this tart as much as I do, and that it wraps around you like the comforting arms of an Italian nonna.

For the Pasta Frolla Pastry

¾ cup (170 g) unsalted butter, room temperature

⅔ cup (80 g) confectioners' sugar

Zest of 1 large orange

1 egg and 1 egg yolk, beaten

3 cups plus 2 tbsp (390 g) all-purpose flour

½ tsp salt

¼ tsp baking powder

To make the pasta frolla pastry, in the bowl of an electric stand mixer fitted with the paddle attachment, cream the butter, confectioners' sugar and orange zest on medium speed until mixed in. Add the beaten egg and egg yolk and mix on low until combined. Scrape down the sides of the bowl. Sift the flour, salt and baking powder into the mixing bowl and mix on low until just combined. Tip the dough onto a lightly floured countertop and press the dough just a couple of times to gather all the crumbs into a ball. Divide the dough in half, and with your hands, lightly shape each half into a disc. Wrap the discs a couple of times with plastic wrap and refrigerate for 1 hour minimum to let the dough rest.

Remove one of the chilled dough discs from the fridge and set it aside on your countertop for 5 minutes to soften slightly. On a lightly floured piece of parchment paper, roll the dough out into a rectangle measuring 17 x 8 inches (43 x 20 cm) so that there is enough dough on all sides to overhang a 14 x 4½-inch (35 x 11–cm) shallow fluted rectangular tart pan with removable base. Flour the base of the tart pan. Please note that this type of dough is prone to breaking, but it is also very easy to patch up. With a pair of sharp scissors, cut straight through the dough and parchment paper to cut your rectangle in half. (Bear with me—I find this method of getting this tricky-to-handle dough into this long tart pan the easiest.)

Pick up one half of the parchment paper and slide that half of the dough into the tart pan so that it hangs over the sides and one end. Repeat this with the remaining half. Let the two pieces meet in the middle of the pan, overlapping slightly. Use your fingers to push the dough up the sides of the pan and press along the edges to trim the dough and remove the excess. Press the center to join together. For any tears in the dough in the tart pan, use your fingers to press it together or add a little extra dough and firm up the sides of the pan and the base. The dough is very forgiving in this way, and you won't see the patches once baked. Refrigerate the prepared tart shell for at least 1 hour to allow the dough to relax further.

(continued)

For the Mixed Berry Jam

2 cups (300 g) blueberries

2 cups (280 g) blackberries

2 cups (330 g) hulled and quartered strawberries

1½ cups (300 g) granulated sugar

3 tbsp (45 ml) fresh lemon juice

Zest of 1 large lemon

¼ cup (60 ml) fresh orange juice

Zest of 1 large orange

For the Topping

1 small egg white

1 tbsp (15 ml) milk

1 tbsp (15 g) coarse turbinado sugar

Thyme leaves, to decorate

Crème fraîche

Tip: A 9-inch (23-cm) round shallow fluted tart pan with removable base can be used instead of a rectangular tart pan for this recipe. Both dough discs will need to be rolled out to 12 inches (30 cm) in diameter.

While the tart shell is chilling, make the mixed fruit jam. Place a small plate in the freezer. In a large heavy-based saucepan, add the blueberries, blackberries, strawberries, sugar, lemon juice and zest and orange juice and zest. Stir together. Bring to a rolling boil over medium-high heat, and then reduce the heat to medium. Add a candy thermometer and cook, uncovered, stirring frequently, until the jam has thickened and the temperature reaches a 215°F (105°C) setting point. Mash the berries after you add the thermometer, or if you prefer large fruit chunks, leave them as they are.

Once the jam reaches the correct temperature, perform the jam setting test. Remove the plate from the freezer and place a dollop of jam onto it. Leave it for a couple of minutes, and then run your finger through the jam. If it wrinkles and stays apart, the jam is ready. If not, continue to boil, and then repeat the test. Once the jam is ready, pour it into a medium bowl and allow to cool completely. It will continue to thicken as it cools. This makes approximately 2⅓ cups (750 g) of jam.

Once the jam is cool, preheat the oven to 350°F (180°C).

Remove the tart shell from the fridge and prick the base of the dough with the tines of a fork. Fill the tart shell with the cooled jam, spreading it out evenly and leaving a small gap at the top edge of the tart shell. Return the base to the fridge while you prepare the lattice. Any leftover jam can be stored in the fridge for up to 2 weeks.

Remove the remaining dough disc from the fridge and transfer it to a clean, lightly floured countertop. Allow the dough to soften slightly, and then roll the dough out to a thickness of ¼ inch (6 mm). Cut the dough into 16 strips measuring ½ x 8 inches (1.3 x 20 cm). Place half of the strips diagonally on top of the jam filling, facing the same direction, to form the bottom half of your lattice. Leave a ½-inch (1.3-cm) gap between each strip. Then, add the remaining strips diagonally, facing the opposite way on top of the first strips so that you form a diamond lattice finish. Use your fingers to press the overhanging dough onto the tart pan to trim. Make an egg wash by whisking together the egg and milk in a small bowl. Brush the lattice lightly with the egg wash and sprinkle with turbinado sugar. Bake for 25 to 30 minutes, or until golden. Remove the crostata from the oven and allow to cool completely on a wire rack before removing it from the tart pan and slicing to serve. Sprinkle thyme leaves to decorate and serve with a dollop of crème fraîche. This crostata can be stored at room temperature in an airtight container for up to 2 days or in the fridge for up to 5 days.

PEAR, GINGER AND HAZELNUT TARTE TATIN

Yield: 1 *(9-inch [23-cm]) tart (8–10 slices)*

A delicious caramel-topped French dessert, tarte Tatin is a treat we all know to be made with apples. Yes, they are delicious in their own right, but this dessert lends itself to using many other fruits such as figs, bananas or peaches. At home we've even made a savory version with caramelized onions and carrots (but that's a whole different cookbook!). My recipe uses pears to sit on that divinely flaky puff pastry and a caramel that is infused with warming stem ginger (candied ginger packaged in jars of its own syrup) and crunchy hazelnuts. If I close my eyes I'm transported to a French café, watching the passersby, enjoying a slice of this delightful treat topped with a scoop of vanilla ice cream.

5–6 pears (750 g)

1 tbsp (15 ml) fresh lemon juice

⅔ cup (130 g) granulated sugar

⅓ cup (75 g) unsalted butter

1 tsp stem ginger

2 tsp (10 ml) stem ginger syrup

1 tsp vanilla bean paste

½ tsp salt

½ cup (60 g) peeled and halved roasted hazelnuts

1 (13-oz [375-g]) puff pastry block, store-bought

Ice cream, to serve

Core the pears, and then peel them as neatly as possible and halve. In a large bowl, pour the lemon juice over the pears and toss to coat to stop them from browning. Set aside. Add the sugar and butter to a 9-inch (23-cm)-wide ovenproof frying pan or skillet and cook over medium heat, without stirring, until it begins to liquefy. As the pan starts to heat, shake to keep the contents from sticking and catching. If the sugar hardens, keep it on low heat for it to gradually melt again. When the butter and sugar have melted and start to brown, give it one good stir with a whisk to avoid any sugar clumps, and then remove from the heat. Add the stem ginger, stem ginger syrup, vanilla bean paste and salt to the frying pan and whisk in. Add the pears and toss gently until coated. Position the pear halves chopped side facing up in the pan in the melted mixture. Position them with the wider side on the edge and the skinnier stem end facing inward. Place two halves in the center of the frying pan. Sprinkle hazelnuts into the gaps around the pears. Return to medium heat and cook for 5 to 10 minutes until the caramel is amber in color and the pears are tender but still firm. Remove from the heat and allow the pears to cool for 30 minutes.

Preheat the oven to 400°F (200°C).

Roll out the puff pastry to about ¼ inch (6 mm) thick and cut a disc measuring 11 inches (28 cm) or slightly bigger than your pan. Place the sheet of pastry over the pears and gently tuck the edges inside the edge of the frying pan. I use a spoon to tuck in the pastry. Using a sharp knife, pierce the pastry in the center to create steam vents. Place the pan on a baking sheet and bake for 35 to 40 minutes, or until the pastry is puffed and golden. Remove from the oven and let cool in the frying pan for 10 minutes. Run a knife around the edge, place a large plate over the top and carefully turn the tart onto the plate. Serve warm with ice cream. This tarte Tatin is best eaten on the same day, as the moisture of the pears will gradually make the crispy puff pastry soggy.

APPLE FENNEL SALTED CARAMEL TART

Yield: 1 (9-inch [23-cm]) tart (10-12 slices)

Apple tart was definitely a dessert that my twin brother and I had on repeat growing up with a French mum. She would make it from memory with a sweet shortcrust pastry and a double hit of apple between an apple purée layer and the (essential!) topping of thinly sliced apples taking center stage. The traditional way of baking it is exceptional, there's no denying that, but I wanted to play around with the flavor combinations to give it my own spin. Caramel and apple go super well together, as do apple and fennel. Yet fennel is used more in savory dishes. That needs to change right away! The fennel caramel here is sublime. It's so unique in its taste, and when set alongside the sweet apples? Oh, my goodness. Awesome! I urge you to try it. It'll blow your mind!

For the Sweet Shortcrust Pastry
1¾ cups (220 g) all-purpose flour
⅓ cup (40 g) confectioners' sugar
¼ tsp salt
½ cup (115 g) cold unsalted butter, chopped into small cubes
1 large egg, cold and beaten
1–2 tbsp (15–30 ml) ice-cold water

To make the sweet shortcrust pastry, in a large mixing bowl, sift the flour, confectioners' sugar and salt. Add the butter and toss until the cubes are coated. Rub the mixture together between your fingers until it reaches a breadcrumb consistency with a few hazelnut-sized pieces of butter still visible. Make a well in the center and add the egg. Using a fork, mix the egg into the flour. Add 1 tablespoon (15 ml) of the ice-cold water, and use your fingertips to bring the dough together. If the dough isn't clumping together, add more water sparingly. Tip the dough onto a lightly floured countertop, and use floured hands to shape the dough into a ball, taking care not to overwork it. Flatten slightly into a disc, and wrap well in plastic wrap. Place in the fridge for at least 1 hour to let the dough rest.

Remove the chilled dough disc from the fridge and set it aside on your countertop for 5 to 10 minutes to allow the dough to warm up slightly so it's easier to roll out. Trying to roll dough that is too cold will cause the edges to crack. To roll out, lightly flour your countertop and rolling pin, and using firm, even strokes, roll from the center outward, turning the dough a quarter turn every few strokes. Roll the dough out to the thickness of a coin (⅛ inch (3 mm) thick) and into a 12-inch (30-cm) circle. Flour the base of a 9-inch (23-cm) shallow fluted tart pan with a removable base, and gently lift the dough and place into the prepared pan. Use your fingers to push the dough up the sides of the pan and into the grooves. Using a sharp knife, trim off the excess dough from the rim. Refrigerate the prepared tart shell for at least 1 hour to allow the dough to relax further. My preference is to leave the shell overnight in the fridge and continue with the recipe the next day. If you do this, cover it well in plastic wrap to ensure that the dough doesn't dry out.

Preheat the oven to 350°F (180°C).

(continued)

For the Fennel Caramel Sauce

3 tbsp (12 g) fennel seeds

1 cup (200 g) granulated sugar

½ cup (115 g) unsalted butter, room temperature and chopped

⅔ cup (160 ml) heavy cream, room temperature

1 tsp vanilla extract

1 tsp natural sea salt flakes (or to taste)

For the Apple Filling

Juice from 1 lemon

5 large apples (about 570 g)

1 tbsp (8 g) confectioners' sugar

Vanilla ice cream, to serve

Once the dough is chilled, prick the tart base all over with a fork, and then line with parchment paper and fill with pie weights all the way up the sides. Blind bake for 15 minutes, and then remove the parchment paper and pie weights. Return the tart back to the oven and bake for 7 to 10 minutes, or until the base is dry and a light golden color. Remove from the oven, and leave the tart shell to cool while you make the caramel and prepare the filling.

To make the fennel caramel sauce, in a small skillet over low heat, lightly toast the fennel seeds. Once fragrant and lightly browned, add to a pestle and mortar and grind to a powder. Set aside. In a high-sided nonstick saucepan, heat the sugar over medium heat, stirring often. Once the sugar is in liquid form, stop stirring and just swirl the liquid sugar as the color changes to a lovely amber color. Keep an eagle eye on it at this stage, as it can turn to burnt sugar very quickly. Carefully add the butter in one go. It will bubble up, but whisk continuously until it has thoroughly melted. Then remove from the heat.

Add the cream, but be careful, as it will bubble up again; keep whisking and the bubbling will die down. Return it to medium heat, stirring occasionally, so that the caramel can thicken. This takes about 5 minutes. Remove from the heat, stir in the ground fennel seeds (add half if you want a more subtle flavor), vanilla extract and salt, and stir thoroughly to combine. Pour into a bowl and set aside to cool for 10 minutes. Pour 1 cup (240 ml) into the bottom of the tart shell and smooth out flat. Pour any remaining caramel into a small serving dish and serve alongside the tart.

To make the apple filling and assemble the tart, add the lemon juice to a large bowl. Cut the apples in half through the core. Remove the core with a sharp knife or melon baller. Slice the apple crossways as thinly as you can. An option is to use a mandoline for this part. Discard (or eat!) the top and bottom of the apple cheeks. Add the apple slices to the bowl and gently toss in the lemon juice to prevent them from browning. Arrange the apple slices into the tart shell in any pattern you desire. I started on the outside of the tart shell and laid them overlapping, continuing in a spiral until the center of the tart. Use your fingers to reposition any if necessary. The thinner the slices, the easier it will be to spiral in the center. Dust with confectioners' sugar.

Place the tart onto a baking sheet and bake in the oven for 30 minutes, until the caramel is bubbling, the apples have softened and the apple edges have caramelized. Cover the edges with foil if the tart shell is browning too quickly and continue to bake. Be careful when removing the tart from the oven, as the caramel will be molten hot and melted to a liquid and the apple slices can slide around. Allow the tart to cool in the tart pan for 15 minutes, repositioning any slices that may have moved when taking the tart out of the oven. After 15 minutes, carefully remove the tart from the pan and slide it onto a serving plate. Serve warm with any remaining caramel sauce drizzled on top and with a scoop of vanilla ice cream. This can be stored at room temperature loosely wrapped in plastic wrap for up to 2 days or in the fridge for up to 4 days.

Tip: Refer to Dark Chocolate Cherry Galette on page 47 for step-by-step images of making sweet shortcrust pastry by hand.

CHOCOLATE PECAN PIE

Yield: 1 (9-inch [23-cm]) tart (10-12 *slices*)

Pecan pie is possibly one of the most nostalgic bakes that can grace a dessert table for many of my American friends across the pond. My version adds chocolate to the filling so that you're left with a gooey, soft, chocolate pecan filling surrounded by super flaky all-butter pastry. This indulgent, extra-tasty pie is perfect for any Thanksgiving table.

For the All-Butter Shortcrust Pastry

1¾ cups (220 g) all-purpose flour

¼ tsp salt

½ cup plus 1 tbsp (130 g) cold unsalted butter, chopped into small cubes

3–4 tbsp (45–60 ml) ice-cold water, plus more if needed

1 small egg

1 tbsp (15 ml) milk

To make the all-butter shortcrust pastry, into a large mixing bowl, sift the flour and salt. Add the butter and toss until the cubes are coated. Rub the mixture together between your fingers until it reaches a breadcrumb consistency with a few walnut half–sized pieces of butter still visible. Add the water, and use your fingertips to bring the dough together. If the dough isn't clumping together, add more water sparingly. Tip the dough onto a lightly floured countertop and use floured hands to shape the dough into a ball, taking care not to overwork it. Flatten the dough slightly into a disc, and wrap well in plastic wrap. Place in the fridge for at least 1 hour to let the dough rest.

Remove the chilled dough disc from the fridge and set it aside on your countertop for 5 to 10 minutes to allow the dough to warm up slightly so it's easier to roll out. Trying to roll dough that is too cold will cause the edges to crack. To roll out, lightly flour your countertop and rolling pin, and using firm, even strokes, roll from the center outward, turning the dough a quarter turn every few strokes. Roll the dough out to the thickness of a coin (⅛ inch [3 mm] thick) and into a 12-inch (30-cm) circle.

Flour the base of a 9-inch (23-cm) shallow fluted tart pan with a removable base, and gently lift the dough and place into the prepared pan. Use your fingers to push the dough up the sides of the pan and into the grooves. Using a sharp knife, trim off the excess dough from the rim. Refrigerate the prepared tart shell for at least 1 hour to allow the dough to relax further. My preference is to leave the shell overnight in the fridge and continue with the recipe the next day. If you do this, cover well in plastic wrap to ensure that the dough doesn't dry out.

Preheat the oven to 350°F (180°C).

(continued)

For the Chocolate Pecan Filling

¼ cup (60 g) unsalted butter

⅔ cup (100 g) chopped 70% dark chocolate

2 tsp (4 g) espresso powder

3 large eggs, room temperature

¾ cup (165 g) firmly packed brown sugar

½ cup (120 ml) maple syrup

2 tbsp (30 ml) molasses

1 tsp vanilla extract

½ tsp salt

⅔ cup (70 g) finely chopped pecan halves

For the Topping

1½ cups (165 g) pecan halves, to decorate

2 tbsp (30 ml) maple syrup

Once the dough is chilled, prick the base all over with a fork, and then line with parchment paper and fill with pie weights all the way up the sides. Blind bake for 15 minutes, and then remove the parchment paper and pie weights. Make an egg wash by whisking together the egg and milk in a small bowl. Brush the base of the tart shell with the egg wash, return it back to the oven and bake for 7 to 10 minutes, or until the base is dry and a light golden color. Remove from the oven and leave the tart shell to cool. Increase the oven temperature to 400°F (200°C).

To make the chocolate pecan filling, melt the butter, chocolate and espresso powder together in a bowl over a pan of simmering water, ensuring the bottom of the bowl does not come into contact with the water. Stir often until melted and smooth. Set aside and allow to cool slightly.

In a large mixing bowl, using handheld electric beaters on medium-high speed, whisk together the eggs, brown sugar, maple syrup, molasses, vanilla and salt until combined. Slowly pour the melted chocolate into the mixture while continuously whisking. Add the finely chopped pecan halves and stir. Pour the filling into the tart shell leaving ¼ inch (6 mm) from the top of the tart shell as allowance for the filling to expand in the oven. Use a spatula to smooth the mixture into an even layer.

Arrange the remaining pecan halves in a circular pattern on top of the pie filling. Cover the edges with foil to prevent browning and remove the foil for the last 15 minutes. Bake the pecan pie for 35 to 40 minutes until the edges are set and the center is still slightly jiggly. The filling may gently puff up, but as it cools, it will settle down. Remove from the oven and cool on a wire rack. Brush the top with the maple syrup while the pie is still warm. This can be stored in the fridge wrapped in plastic wrap for up to 4 days.

Notes: If you don't want to spend the time laying the pecans neatly on the top, chop them coarsely or leave them whole and sprinkle over the filling instead.

You can also use a 9-inch (23-cm) shallow pie dish. When placing the pie dough into the base, you will need to crimp the edges with your fingers.

THE ULTIMATE CHOCOLATE BANOFFEE PIE

Yield: 1 *(9-inch [23-cm]) pie (10-12 slices)*

Banoffee pie is up there as one of the more famous British pie inventions. Ever since my boarding school days where this was a canteen staple, I have loved this dessert. Like truly, madly, deeply loved it! The combination of the biscuit base, caramel, sliced bananas and whipped cream is my kryptonite! Here I've used chocolate sandwich biscuits and added chocolate to the caramel, which I assure you will make this a crowd-pleasing favorite.

For the Chocolate Biscuit Base

3 cups (300 g) chocolate sandwich biscuits (Bourbon biscuits or Oreos® will work well)

½ cup (115 g) unsalted butter

For the Chocolate Caramel Filling

1 (14-oz [307-ml]) can condensed milk

½ cup (115 g) unsalted butter, room temperature

¼ cup (55 g) firmly packed light brown sugar

¼ cup (60 ml) golden syrup

¼ tsp salt

⅔ cup (100 g) finely chopped 70% dark chocolate

For the Topping

⅓ cup (50 g) coarsely chopped 70% dark chocolate, for the curls

2 cups (480 ml) heavy cream, chilled

2 large bananas

Tips: Find chocolate sandwich biscuits at your local grocery store or online.

Use graham crackers or digestive biscuits and omit the chocolate in the caramel for a more traditional banoffee pie. Good quality store-bought caramel can alternatively be used. Dust with cocoa powder rather than decorating with chocolate curls, if desired.

To make the chocolate biscuit base, break the biscuits into chunky pieces and put them into the canister of a food processor. Blend into crumbs. Melt the butter in a small skillet, and then add it to the canister and pulse until well blended and starting to clump. Pour the mixture into the center of a 9-inch (23-cm) shallow fluted tart pan with a removable base. Press the mixture firmly over the base of the pan and up the sides with your fingers or with the bottom of a glass. Transfer the base to the fridge to chill for about 30 minutes, or until firm.

To make the caramel layer, in a medium saucepan over medium heat, add the condensed milk, butter, sugar, golden syrup and salt and heat until the sugar has dissolved. Increase the heat, and bring the mixture to a boil, stirring continuously so that it doesn't catch. The caramel will thicken to a soft fudge consistency and turn golden brown. Be careful to not cook it for too long, otherwise the caramel will turn grainy and separated. Add the chocolate, let it sit for 1 minute and then stir until the chocolate has melted and combined. Take the set biscuit base out of the fridge and pour the hot chocolate caramel into the biscuit base. Smooth with an offset spatula, and then return the base to the fridge for 1 hour to cool completely and chill.

For the topping, make the chocolate curls by melting the chocolate in a bowl set over a pan of simmering water, ensuring the bottom of the bowl does not come into contact with the water. Once melted, spread the chocolate on a clean cookie sheet, in a thin layer. Place the cookie sheet in the fridge to set for 1 hour. Remove from the fridge, and then scrape carefully using a long, sharp knife held at a slight angle, until the chocolate curls up towards you. If the chocolate feels too hard to create the curls, allow the cookie sheet to sit at room temperature for a little while, and then try again. Once the curls are created, put them back in the fridge until needed.

To assemble, pour the cream into a large bowl, whip with electric handheld beaters until thickened but not stiff and set to one side. When ready to serve, slice the bananas and layer them over the set caramel. Spoon the cream over the bananas using the back of your spoon to create swirls. Then top with chocolate curls. Serve immediately. This can be stored in the fridge wrapped loosely in plastic wrap for 3 to 4 days.

MEMORY-MAKING CAKES

Cake features prominently in some shape or form in so many of our earliest childhood memories. From simple cupcakes slathered in buttercream and covered in sprinkles and beautifully designed wedding cakes to cakes shared at gatherings with our closest family members, we've all felt the love of cakes and their ability to take us on a trip down memory lane.

I've started this chapter with a twist on the classic chocolate cupcake. Adding rosemary-infused buttercream and candied pecans gives Double Chocolate Cupcakes with Rosemary Buttercream (page 73) a facelift like no other. If you haven't tried rosemary and chocolate before . . . run, don't walk to the kitchen and get baking!

I also share some everyday family favorites like the Springtime Lemon and Thyme Drizzle Cake (page 79), Chocolate Orange Marble Loaf with Chocolate Ganache (page 80) and the Sour Cream Blackberry Cake Your Nana Would Love (page 89). These are cakes designed to bake easily, so they don't require hours in the kitchen but are still undoubtedly delicious.

The chapter includes a series of cakes meant for gatherings and celebrations. From the Epic Birthday Espresso Crêpes Cake (page 75) to the Pavlova with Pomegranate Poached Pears (page 83), you will stun your crowd when you produce these beauties. Last but by no means least is the retro classic Showstopper Black Forest Layer Cake (page 94), which I've kept true to itself. Sometimes a classic is perfect just the way it is.

DOUBLE CHOCOLATE CUPCAKES WITH ROSEMARY BUTTERCREAM

Yield: **12 *cupcakes***

Cupcakes are the ultimate kids' treat, am I right? Soft, fluffy sponge topped with sweet buttercream and a smattering of sprinkles. Kid heaven. But why not create a cupcake for the grown-ups to enjoy, too? Rosemary is infused into the butter prior to making your buttercream, and this simple addition provides an excitingly sophisticated edge. Maple-candied pecans provide textural crunch atop the fluffy buttercream and rich, indulgent sponge. Kids, hands off . . . this one's ours!

For the Rosemary Buttercream

1½ cups (345 g) unsalted butter, room temperature, divided

4 sprigs fresh rosemary, 4" (10 cm) long, plus extra for garnishing (optional)

3½ cups (420 g) confectioners' sugar

1 tbsp (15 ml) heavy cream

1 tsp vanilla extract

¼ tsp salt

For the Chocolate Cupcakes

½ cup (115 g) unsalted butter, room temperature

½ cup (100 g) granulated sugar

¼ cup (55 g) firmly packed light brown sugar

2 large eggs, room temperature

1 tsp vanilla extract

1 cup (125 g) all-purpose flour

½ cup (45 g) unsweetened cocoa powder

1 tsp baking powder

½ tsp baking soda

½ tsp salt

½ cup (120 ml) sour cream, room temperature

½ cup (75 g) coarsely chopped milk chocolate

To start the rosemary buttercream, in a small saucepan over medium heat, melt ¾ cup (170 g) of the butter. Add the rosemary and cook for 5 minutes on low heat. Transfer the melted butter and the rosemary to a bowl and let it steep at room temperature for at least 3 hours. Strain out the rosemary and transfer the infused rosemary butter to the fridge to resolidify. This step can be done the day before making the cupcakes.

Preheat the oven to 350°F (180°C), and line a 12-well cupcake pan with cupcake liners.

To make the chocolate cupcakes, beat the butter, granulated sugar and brown sugar in the bowl of an electric stand mixer fitted with the paddle attachment on medium speed for about 5 minutes, or until light and creamy. Add the eggs one at a time and the vanilla, beating well after each addition. Ensure that you scrape down the sides and bottom of the bowl. In a separate bowl, sift the flour, cocoa powder, baking powder, baking soda and salt and stir to combine. Turn the mixer to low speed and add half of the dry ingredients to the batter mixing until just combined. Add the sour cream and mix, and then add the remaining dry ingredients and milk chocolate and mix until only a few streaks of flour remain, being careful not to overmix.

(continued)

For the Candied Pecans

1 cup (110 g) pecans halves

2 tbsp (30 ml) maple syrup

1 tsp vanilla extract

½ tsp flaked sea salt

Divide the batter equally between the 12 cupcake liners. Bake for 15 to 18 minutes, or until the center of the cupcake springs back up if gently pressed and a toothpick comes out clean. Remove the cupcakes from the oven and cool in the pan for 5 to 10 minutes before turning out on a wire rack to cool completely.

While the oven is still on, make the candied pecans. Mix the pecans, maple syrup and vanilla in a small bowl until the nuts are fully coated. Lay them on a baking sheet lined with parchment paper and bake for 15 minutes, tossing halfway through. Remove the baking sheet from the oven, sprinkle the candied pecans with sea salt, toss to coat and then allow to cool completely before chopping coarsely.

When the infused butter has solidified to a room temperature consistency, it's time to finish the buttercream. (If the rosemary butter becomes too solid, remove it from the fridge and allow it to soften to room temperature.) In the bowl of an electric stand mixer fitted with the paddle attachment, add the infused butter and remaining butter, and beat on medium speed for about 8 minutes, or until smooth and light. Scrape down the bowl and beat in the confectioners' sugar. Add the cream, vanilla and salt, and beat for another 3 to 4 minutes, or until the buttercream is light and fluffy.

Spoon the buttercream into a piping bag fitted with your favorite piping tip and pipe buttercream onto each cupcake. Sprinkle the cupcakes with candied pecans, and decorate with a sprig of rosemary, if desired. These can be stored at room temperature in an airtight container for up to 2 days or in the fridge for up to 5 days.

EPIC BIRTHDAY ESPRESSO CRÊPES CAKE

Yield: **1 *(9-inch [23-cm]) cake (16–20 slices)***

When my daughter, Lani, turned seven, we had extended family over to celebrate for breakfast. I didn't want to make a traditional birthday cake to eat at that time in the morning, so I combined two breakfast favorites—crêpes and coffee—and made her a crêpes layer cake with coffee whipped cream. We all loved it, and I am so excited to share with you an updated version with the addition of espresso caramel sauce (game changer!). This beautiful cake is EPIC in so many ways. Sure it takes time to make all those crêpes, but it's totally worth it. Plus, it feeds a lot of people, which is perfect for a gathering. It keeps for quite a few days, and the recipe can also be scaled down easily if you prefer a smaller version.

For the Crêpes

3 cups (375 g) all-purpose flour

¼ cup (50 g) granulated sugar

½ tsp salt

⅓ cup (75 g) unsalted butter

9 large eggs, room temperature

4½ cups (1.1 L) whole milk

½ cup (120 ml) cold water

2 tsp (10 ml) vanilla extract

For the Espresso Chocolate Whipped Cream

6 cups (1.4 L) heavy cream

1¼ cups (150 g) confectioners' sugar

½ cup plus 2 tbsp (55 g) unsweetened cocoa powder

¼ cup (15 g) espresso powder

¼ tsp salt

To make the crêpes, in a large bowl, sift the flour, sugar and salt. Mix and set aside. In a saucepan, melt the butter over medium heat. In a medium bowl, whisk together the eggs, milk, water, melted butter and vanilla until combined. Slowly pour the wet ingredients mixture into the dry ingredients, whisking continuously. Whisk until any lumps have disappeared and the batter is smooth. Set aside for 1 hour in the fridge to allow the batter to rest.

Heat a lightly oiled 9-inch (23-cm) pancake pan or nonstick frying pan over medium-high heat. Whisk the batter before pouring ¼ cup (60 ml) of batter into the pan. Tip and rotate the pan to spread the batter as thinly as possible all around. If there are any holes in the crêpe, just fill them in with a bit of batter. Cook for about 45 seconds until the underside is golden and flip over gently using a rubber spatula. Cook the second side for another 20 seconds, and then gently slide the crêpe onto a plate and start the process again. Ensure that you whisk the batter before making another crêpe. As the batter gets to the end, it can become a bit thicker; if so, whisk in a couple of tablespoons (30 ml) of milk to thin it out. Keep making crêpes until all the batter is gone. You will get 30 to 34 crêpes out of your batter depending on how thin you have made them.

To prepare the espresso chocolate whipped cream, add the cream, confectioners' sugar, cocoa powder, espresso powder and salt into the bowl of an electric stand mixer fitted with the whisk attachment. Whip the cream until soft peaks form. Refrigerate until needed.

(continued)

For the Espresso Caramel Sauce

1 cup (200 g) granulated sugar

½ cup (115 g) unsalted butter, room temperature and chopped

⅔ cup (160 ml) heavy cream, room temperature

2 tsp (4 g) espresso powder

1 tsp vanilla extract

1 tsp natural sea salt flakes

For Serving

1 tbsp (8 g) confectioners' sugar

Fresh figs, quartered

To make the espresso caramel, in a high-sided nonstick saucepan, heat the sugar over medium heat, stirring often with a wooden spoon. The sugar will soon start to clump, but continue to stir, and after a minute or so the sugar clumps will turn into liquid. Once the sugar is in liquid form, stop stirring and swirl the liquid sugar as the color changes to a lovely amber. Keep an eagle eye on it at this stage as it can turn to burnt sugar very quickly. Remove the saucepan from the heat and add the butter. It will bubble up, but return the pan to medium heat and whisk the butter in until it has thoroughly melted. Remove from the heat and add the cream and espresso powder. Again, it will bubble up, but keep whisking and the bubbling will die down. Put the caramel back on medium heat and leave it, stirring occasionally, so that the caramel can thicken. This takes about 5 minutes. Remove from the heat, stir in the vanilla and sea salt flakes and leave to cool slightly in the pan before pouring into a pitcher or measuring cup.

To assemble, place one crêpe on a cutting board or plate and spread over a little of the espresso chocolate whipped cream with a spatula. I measured ¼ cup (60 ml) of whipped cream each time to keep the layers equal. Place a second crêpe onto this layer of cream. Repeat, layering crêpes and cream, until the crêpes have been used up, finishing with a crêpe on the top. Refrigerate for 1 hour to allow the cream to set. When ready to serve, dust with confectioners' sugar and top with candles and fresh flowers, if you'd like. Serve a slice of crêpes layer cake with a drizzle of espresso caramel sauce and quartered fresh figs. This can be kept in the fridge wrapped in plastic wrap for up to 4 days.

Notes: The espresso powder can be omitted from the whipped cream and from the caramel sauce if desired.

This is a large cake that serves many. If you would like a smaller cake, halve the crêpes and the whipped cream ingredients and continue with the method as normal. You will then make a 15-layer crêpes cake that serves 10 to 12 instead. Keep the caramel ingredients the same, and any remaining caramel can be refrigerated to be enjoyed on ice cream at a later date!

Leave a ½-inch (1.3-cm) gap from the edge of the crêpes when spreading the cream. When adding each new crêpe layer, gently press down to level it, and push out the cream to the edge.

SPRINGTIME LEMON AND THYME DRIZZLE CAKE

Yield: 1 *(9 x 5–inch [23 x 13-cm]) loaf (8–10 slices)*

The classic lemon drizzle cake is often a family favorite, and deservedly so. With a lovely buttery, light, moist sponge and the zingy lemon syrup and sweet-yet-tangy glaze, you can understand why this classic recipe gets passed down from generation to generation. I've included fresh thyme leaves in the batter to provide a subtle-but-effective change to the original drizzle cake and baked it in a stunning decorative loaf pan for that extra wow factor.

For the Lemon Cake

1 cup (230 g) unsalted butter, room temperature, plus more melted for greasing

1¾ cups (220 g) all-purpose flour, plus more for dusting (optional)

1 cup (200 g) granulated sugar

Zest of 2 large lemons

3 large eggs, room temperature

1 tsp baking powder

¼ tsp salt

1 tbsp (2 g) roughly chopped fresh thyme leaves, plus extra leaves for garnishing (optional)

For the Lemon Syrup

⅓ cup (65 g) granulated sugar

⅓ cup (80 ml) fresh lemon juice (about 2 lemons)

For the Lemon Glaze

1 cup (120 g) confectioners' sugar

2 tbsp (30 ml) fresh lemon juice, plus extra if necessary

Tip: To make a thicker glaze, whisk in only 1 tablespoon (15 ml) of lemon juice. I used a thin glaze to highlight the shape of the decorative loaf pan.

Preheat the oven to 350°F (180°C). Grease a 9 x 5–inch (23 x 13–cm) loaf pan with melted butter. If using a decorative loaf pan, place the pan in the fridge for 10 minutes to allow the butter to harden. Afterwards, dust with flour, tapping any excess out. If using a standard loaf pan, grease and line with parchment paper.

To make the lemon cake, in a small bowl, combine the sugar and lemon zest, and using your fingertips, rub the two together for 1 minute to release the oils of the zest into the sugar. In the bowl of an electric mixer fitted with the paddle attachment, cream the butter and lemon and sugar mixture on medium speed for 5 minutes, or until pale. Reduce the speed to low, and add the eggs one at a time, beating well after each addition until well incorporated. Ensure that you scrape down the sides of the bowl.

In a separate bowl, sift the flour, baking powder and salt, and then stir to combine. Add the prepared flour mix and thyme leaves to the mixer bowl, and beat on low until just combined. Pour the batter into the prepared loaf pan and smooth the top. Bake for 40 to 45 minutes, or until golden and a toothpick inserted into the center comes out clean. Remove from the oven and allow the cake to cool in the loaf pan for 10 minutes. Then invert onto a wire rack and remove the pan.

While the cake is in the oven, make the lemon syrup. Combine the sugar and lemon juice in a small saucepan, and stir over medium heat until the sugar is dissolved. Remove from the heat. Once the cake is inverted from the pan onto a wire rack, prick the warm cake all over with a skewer and pour the syrup over it. Allow the cake to cool completely.

To make the lemon glaze, use a fine-mesh sieve to sift the confectioners' sugar into a medium bowl. Whisk in the lemon juice until you have a smooth, thin glaze. If the glaze is too thick, add more lemon juice or water, 1 teaspoon at a time until you've reached your desired consistency. Drizzle the glaze over the top of the cooled cake and sprinkle with extra thyme leaves. This can be stored at room temperature in an airtight container for up to 4 days or in the freezer for 1 month.

CHOCOLATE ORANGE MARBLE LOAF WITH CHOCOLATE GANACHE

Yield: 1 *(9 x 5–inch [23 x 13–cm]) loaf (8–10 slices)*

In this recipe, a good ol' fashioned marble cake is given a makeover with the addition of orange . . . because chocolate and orange are like two best friends. They work hand in hand perfectly. Chocolate and orange is my all-time favorite flavor combination, and this loaf has it in spades. The luxurious chocolate ganache layer takes decadence to the max, making this a scrumptious bite to eat.

For the Marbled Loaf

1 cup (230 g) unsalted butter, room temperature

1 cup (200 g) granulated sugar

3 large eggs, room temperature

1¾ cups (220 g) all-purpose flour

1 tsp baking powder

½ tsp baking soda

¼ tsp salt

¼ cup (60 ml) whole milk

2 tsp (10 ml) orange extract

Zest of 1 large orange, plus extra for garnishing (optional)

2 tbsp (30 ml) fresh orange juice

3 tbsp (16 g) unsweetened cocoa powder

Preheat the oven to 350°F (180°C). Grease and line the base of a 9 x 5–inch (23 x 13–cm) loaf pan with parchment paper.

To make the marbled loaf, in the bowl of an electric mixer fitted with the paddle attachment, cream the butter and sugar on medium speed for 5 minutes, or until pale. Reduce the speed to low, and add the eggs one at a time, beating well after each addition until well incorporated. Ensure that you scrape down the sides of the bowl. In a separate bowl, sift the flour, baking powder, baking soda and salt, and stir to combine. Add this mixture to the batter and mix on low until just combined. Add the milk and mix again until just incorporated.

Separate the batter equally into two bowls. In one bowl, add the orange extract and orange zest and stir to combine. In the other bowl, add the orange juice and cocoa powder and stir to combine. You now have two separate batters, one plain orange and one chocolate orange batter.

Spoon the batter into the prepared loaf pan by spreading a layer of the plain orange batter on the bottom and leveling it out with the back of a spoon. Then layer the chocolate orange batter, and alternate between the two until all the batter is used. Level off the top with a butter knife and swirl the knife through the batter to create a ripple effect. Be careful not to over swirl, as the batter will all mix together. Bake for 40 to 50 minutes, or until a toothpick inserted into the center comes out clean. Remove the loaf from the oven and allow it to cool in the pan for 10 minutes. Then invert onto a wire rack and cool completely.

(continued)

For the Chocolate Ganache
½ cup (120 ml) heavy cream
1¼ cups (185 g) coarsely chopped 70% dark chocolate
1 tbsp (15 ml) golden syrup

Tip: This is lovely and orangey, but if you prefer, you can add just 1 teaspoon of orange extract or leave it out altogether for a softer orange flavor.

While the marble loaf is cooling, make the chocolate ganache. In a small saucepan over medium heat, heat the cream until hot and bubbling at the edges, but do not allow it to boil. Place the chopped chocolate into a bowl, pour the hot cream over the chocolate and leave it to stand for 5 minutes. Add the golden syrup, and stir until the chocolate has fully melted and combined. Set aside for 15 minutes or so to thicken and cool to room temperature. You want the ganache to cool and thicken sufficiently so that when poured it holds on top of the loaf. Spoon half of the ganache over the top of the marble loaf. Decorate with some orange zest, if desired, and then slice and serve with the remaining chocolate ganache. Over time, the ganache will harden completely. Any remaining ganache can be heated gently in the microwave to make it a spoonable consistency again. This loaf can be kept in an airtight container at room temperature for up to 2 days or in the fridge for 4 to 5 days.

PAVLOVA WITH POMEGRANATE POACHED PEARS

Yield: 1 *(9-inch [23-cm]) meringue (10-12 slices)*

Having spent fifteen years living in Australia, I quickly learned the mighty fruit Pavlova would grace our table on many occasions, big and small. Whether it was a full-blown gathering on Australia Day or a quiet lunch with the family, some of my fondest memories living in beautiful Sydney were spent enjoying Pavlova. Here, meringue with a crisp outer shell and pillowy soft center, topped with whipped cream, is given an autumnal touch with pomegranate poached pears. The poaching liquid is then reduced to create a pomegranate caramel, resulting in a sweet-yet-tart sauce full of complexities that sits wonderfully alongside the meringue.

For the Pavlova

5 large egg whites

1¼ cups (250 g) superfine caster sugar

1 tsp fresh lemon juice

1 tsp cornstarch

Preheat the oven to 275°F (135°C). Line a baking sheet with parchment paper and trace a 9-inch (23-cm) diameter circle. This circle should be smaller than the plate or cake stand on which you are serving your Pavlova. Turn the parchment paper over so that the pen/pencil line is underneath.

To make the Pavlova, in the bowl of an electric stand mixer fitted with the whisk attachment, whisk the egg whites on medium speed until soft peaks form when the whisk is removed, about 5 minutes. As you whisk, gradually add the sugar one spoonful at a time whisking well between each spoonful. Once all the sugar is added, whisk in the lemon juice and cornstarch, and continue to whisk for 5 minutes. By now, the mixture should be thick and glossy, and the sugar should be fully incorporated. If you rub a bit of mixture between your thumb and finger, there should be no grit as the sugar should be fully blended. If there is still some grit, continuing whipping for a couple of minutes.

Dab a small amount of the meringue under the corners of the prepared parchment paper and press down onto the baking sheet. This secures the paper and prevents it from slipping in the next step. Scoop the meringue mixture onto the lined baking sheet into the circle that you've drawn. Then spread out the meringue with a spatula to create a large meringue nest with soft peaks rising all around.

Place the baking sheet in the center of the oven, immediately reduce the oven temperature to 225°F (110°C) and bake for 2½ hours. Then, turn the oven off and leave it in the oven with the door closed for a minimum of 2 hours (preferably overnight), to cool completely. Do not open the door during the cooking or cooling process as this lets in moisture. I always make my Pavlova the evening before I want to serve it so that the cooling time happens overnight. Just don't forget in the morning that it's in the oven!

(continued)

For the Pomegranate Poached Pears

2½ cups (600 ml) pomegranate juice

½ cup (100 g) granulated sugar

1 vanilla pod, sliced in half lengthways

Peel of 1 large orange

¼ cup (60 ml) fresh orange juice

1 star anise

1 cinnamon stick

½ tsp ground ginger

5 pears, Bosc or Conference

½ cup (110 g) firmly packed brown sugar

½ cup (120 ml) heavy cream

2 tbsp (30 g) unsalted butter

For Assembling

1½ cups (360 ml) heavy cream

3 tbsp (55 g) pomegranate arils

One hour prior to serving the Pavlova, make the poached pears and pomegranate caramel. In a large saucepan over medium-high heat, add the pomegranate juice, granulated sugar, vanilla pod, orange peel, orange juice, star anise, cinnamon stick and ground ginger. Bring this poaching liquid to a boil, stirring continuously, until the sugar has dissolved. Peel the pears, leaving them whole with the stems on, but remove the core with a melon baller. (Alternatively, slice them in half but note that the poaching time may need to be reduced.) Once at a rolling boil, reduce the heat of the poaching liquid to medium-low and add the pears into the saucepan. The liquid should just cover their tops. Simmer for 10 to 15 minutes, or until the pears are tender. The timing will depend on the size and ripeness of the pears. Flip the pears over halfway through. When the pears are soft, remove them from the saucepan using a slotted spoon and allow them to cool slightly.

Bring the heat back up to medium-high and boil for 10 to 15 minutes to reduce the liquid. Once it has reduced to about 1 cup (240 ml), remove any solids with a slotted spoon. Reduce the heat to low, add the brown sugar, cream and butter, and let simmer uncovered for about 10 to 15 minutes. It will turn into a slightly thickened, caramel-colored sauce. Remove from the heat and set aside. The sauce will continue to thicken as it cools.

For assembly, place the cream in the bowl of a stand mixer fitted with the whisk attachment and whip until soft peaks form. Add 3 tablespoons (45 ml) of the cooled pomegranate caramel sauce and ripple throughout.

Gently place the meringue onto the serving plate. Dollop cream onto the top of the meringue base. Top with poached pears and spoon some of the caramel sauce onto the pears. Scatter with pomegranate arils. Serve immediately with an extra drizzle of caramel, slicing the pears accordingly. This is definitely best when eaten on the same day, but any remaining Pavlova can be kept in the fridge wrapped in plastic wrap for 24 hours.

Tips: Don't worry if your Pavlova cracks. You can still serve it, as any cracks will be hidden under the cream and pears. Alternatively, break it up into individual pieces, top with cream, caramel sauce, sliced pears and pomegranate jewels, and you have yourself an Eton mess. It tastes exactly the same!

The bowl in which you whip your egg whites for the Pavlova should be free of grease and totally dry. Also, moisture in the air will cause your egg whites to collapse. Ensure that you can feel no sugar grains between your fingers once the sugar is whipped in.

ORANGE AND ALMOND SEMOLINA CAKE

Yield: **1** *(8-inch [20-cm]) cake (10-12 slices)*

I first ate an almond semolina cake when visiting my pen pal in Monaco one summer. The light, nutty, moist texture of that cake has always stayed with me. The flavors of orange, almond, pistachios and figs feel ever so Italian to me, most likely due to Monaco's proximity to the Italian border. With these flavors combined within this simple cake, served with the Greek yogurt and orange honey syrup, you'll be taken aback by just how beautifully delicious it is.

For the Orange Almond Semolina Cake

⅔ cup (130 g) granulated sugar

Zest of 2 large oranges

¾ cup (170 g) unsalted butter, room temperature

3 large eggs, room temperature

1½ cups (150 g) almond meal

¾ cup (120 g) semolina

1 tsp baking powder

1 tbsp (15 ml) orange blossom water

⅓ cup (80 ml) Greek yogurt

For the Orange Honey Syrup

⅓ cup (80 ml) fresh orange juice

2 tbsp (30 ml) runny honey

2 tbsp (30 g) firmly packed light brown sugar

For the Topping

½ cup (120 ml) Greek yogurt

¼ cup (25 g) chopped pistachios

2 figs, to serve (optional)

Preheat the oven to 350°F (180°C). Grease the base and sides of an 8-inch (20-cm) cake pan and line with parchment paper.

To make the cake, in a small bowl, combine the sugar and orange zest, and using your fingertips, rub them together for 1 minute to release the oils of the zest into the sugar. In the bowl of an electric mixer fitted with the paddle attachment, cream the butter and orange and sugar mixture on medium speed for 5 minutes, or until pale. Reduce the speed to low and add the eggs one at a time, beating well after each addition until well incorporated. Ensure that you scrape down the sides of the bowl. Add the almond meal, semolina, baking powder, orange blossom water and yogurt into the mixer bowl and beat well to combine. Pour the batter into the prepared cake pan and smooth the top. Bake for 40 to 45 minutes, or until golden and a toothpick inserted into the center comes out clean. Remove from the oven and allow to cool in the pan for 10 minutes before turning out onto a wire rack to cool completely.

While the cake is cooling, make the orange honey syrup. Add the orange juice, honey and brown sugar into a small saucepan and bring to a boil. Boil gently for 5 minutes, and then set aside to cool. The syrup will thicken as it cools.

Once the cake has cooled, spoon the Greek yogurt topping onto the cake and drizzle with the orange syrup. Sprinkle with chopped pistachios and serve with quartered figs, if desired. This can be stored in the fridge for 4 to 5 days.

SOUR CREAM BLACKBERRY CAKE
YOUR NANA WOULD LOVE

Yield: **1** *(8-inch [20-cm]) cake (10-12 slices)*

We should all have that recipe in our repertoire that our nanas would love. Something simple and adaptable that can be made for when your beloved nana might drop by for a cuppa or that you can surprise her with when you visit. This cake is exactly that. A super-tender sour cream cake with the incredible addition of Earl Grey tea in the batter and juicy blackberries throughout. Fragrant, delicate, fruity, this cake has it all. The best part is that you can omit the tea leaves and substitute any fruit you like. This, unquestionably, is one of my family's favorites.

½ cup (115 g) unsalted butter, room temperature

⅔ cup (130 g) granulated sugar

1 tbsp (8 g) ground Earl Grey tea

2 large eggs, room temperature

1¾ cups (220 g) all-purpose flour

1½ tsp (7 g) baking powder

¼ tsp salt

½ cup (120 ml) sour cream

1 tsp vanilla extract

2 cups (280 g) halved fresh blackberries, divided

2 tbsp (30 g) coarse turbinado sugar

1 tsp confectioners' sugar, to dust

Preheat the oven to 350°F (180°C). Grease the base and sides of an 8-inch (20-cm) springform cake pan and line with parchment paper.

In the bowl of an electric stand mixer fitted with the paddle attachment, cream the butter, granulated sugar and tea together on medium speed for 5 minutes, or until pale. Reduce the speed to low and add the eggs one at a time, beating well after each addition until well incorporated. Ensure that you scrape down the sides of the bowl. In a separate bowl, sift the flour, baking powder and salt and mix. Add half of the dry ingredients to the stand mixer bowl and mix on low speed until combined. Add the sour cream and vanilla and mix again. Add the remaining dry ingredients and mix on low speed until everything is incorporated. Reserve one-quarter of the blackberries and add the rest to the batter. Fold through gently.

Pour the batter into the prepared cake pan and dot the remaining blackberries on top (don't push them in, otherwise they tend to sink while baking). Sprinkle the top of the batter and fruit with turbinado sugar. Bake for 50 to 60 minutes, or until golden and a toothpick inserted into the center comes out clean. If the cake starts to brown too much, cover it with foil for the remaining bake time. Remove from the oven and allow to cool in the pan for 10 minutes before turning out onto a wire rack. Dust with confectioner's sugar. This cake is best served warm and with a freshly brewed cup of tea! It can be stored at room temperature in an airtight container for up to 2 days or in the fridge for 4 to 5 days.

Tip: The Earl Grey tea can be left out if preferred. This is a great cake to swap out the blackberries for any other fruit or a combination of various fruits that you may have on hand such as raspberries, strawberries, peaches, plums, blueberries or chopped apples or pears, to name a few.

BANANA WALNUT BUNDT CAKE WITH MAPLE GLAZE

Yield: **12–16** *servings*

Warm banana bread formed a major part of my diet at university, as I'm sure it did for many students! Here I've transformed it into a banana Bundt cake filled with chopped walnuts and topped with the addition of a beautiful maple icing. Perfect to use up those overripe bananas, this buttery tender crumb cake serves a crowd in the easiest way possible.

For the Banana Walnut Cake

1 cup (230 g) unsalted butter, room temperature

1 cup (200 g) granulated sugar

½ cup (110 g) firmly packed brown sugar

2 tsp (10 ml) vanilla extract

3 large eggs, room temperature

3 cups (375 g) all-purpose flour

2 tsp (10 g) baking powder

½ tsp salt

1½ cups (320 g) overripe and mashed bananas (about 3 bananas)

½ cup (120 ml) sour cream

¾ cup (90 g) finely chopped walnut halves

For the Maple Icing

2 cups (240 g) sifted confectioners' sugar, plus more as needed

½ cup (120 g) cream cheese, room temperature

3 tbsp (45 g) unsalted butter, room temperature

2–3 tbsp (30–45 ml) maple syrup

For the Topping

¼ cup (30 g) coarsely chopped walnut halves

¼ cup (30 g) coarsely chopped dried banana chips

Preheat the oven to 350°F (180°C). Thoroughly grease a 10- to 12-cup (2.4- to 2.8-L) Bundt pan. Dust with flour and knock out any excess.

To make the banana walnut cake, in the bowl of an electric stand mixer fitted with the paddle attachment, cream the butter, granulated sugar and brown sugar on medium speed for 5 minutes, or until pale. Reduce the speed to low, add the vanilla, then add the eggs one at a time, beating well after each addition until well incorporated. Ensure that you scrape down the sides of the bowl. In a separate bowl, sift the flour, baking powder and salt and mix. Add half of the dry ingredients into the stand mixer bowl and mix on low speed until combined. Add the mashed bananas and sour cream and mix again. Add the remaining dry ingredients and chopped walnuts and mix until only a few flour streaks remain, ensuring that you don't overmix.

Pour the batter into the prepared pan and smooth the top. Bake for 45 to 55 minutes, or until golden and a toothpick inserted into the center comes out clean. If the cake starts to brown too much, cover with foil for the remaining bake time. Remove from the oven and allow to cool in the pan for 10 minutes before turning out onto a wire rack to cool completely.

To make the maple icing, add the confectioners' sugar, cream cheese, butter and maple syrup to the bowl of an electric stand mixer fitted with the paddle attachment. Blend the ingredients on medium speed. You want the glaze to be thick enough so that it drips down the sides of the cake and holds, but not so thin that it will drip right off the cake. If you find it too thin, add more confectioners' sugar, ¼ cup (30 g) at a time. Spoon the glaze onto the top of the cake and let it ooze down the sides. Sprinkle with chopped walnuts and dried banana chips and allow to set for 15 minutes before slicing and serving. This is best eaten on the same day but can be stored in the fridge wrapped loosely in plastic wrap for up to 2 days. Any remaining slices can be microwaved for 10 to 20 seconds.

Tips: For something different, swap out the walnuts with pecans, hazelnuts or even chopped chocolate.

This recipe can be halved and baked for 40 to 45 minutes in a 9 x 5–inch (23 x 13–cm) loaf pan, greased and lined with parchment paper.

Yield: 1 (9-inch [23-cm]) cheesecake (10-12 slices)

To bake or not to bake? When it comes to cheesecake, it's "not to bake" for me. Made this way, I find a good cheesecake so light and easy to indulge in. The buttery biscuit base is topped with a smooth white chocolate cream cheese filling, which is offset by a fruity, tangy raspberry sauce and extra fresh raspberries, too. I made a version of this cheesecake early on in my marriage with Anthony, and it's been a favorite of ours to make and enjoy together ever since.

For the Biscuit Base

2½ cups (250 g) digestive biscuits or graham crackers pieces

½ cup (115 g) unsalted butter

For the White Chocolate Cheesecake

2 cups (300 g) white chocolate chunks

1 cup (240 ml) heavy cream

2 cups (480 g) cream cheese, softened and at room temperature

¼ cup (50 g) granulated sugar

½ cup (60 g) sifted confectioners' sugar

1 tsp vanilla bean paste

For the Raspberry Sauce

⅓ cup (65 g) granulated sugar

1 tbsp (8 g) cornstarch

¼ cup (60 ml) fresh lemon juice

3 cups (370 g) fresh or frozen raspberries

For Serving

½ cup (60 g) fresh raspberries

½ cup (80 g) sliced fresh strawberries

¼ cup (25 g) fresh red currants

Tip: Wipe the blade of the knife after each cut so that the edges of the cheesecake slices remain clean.

To make the biscuit base, grease the bottom and sides of a 9-inch (23-cm) springform pan, and line the base with parchment paper. Place the biscuit pieces into the canister of a food processor. Blend into crumbs. Melt the butter in a saucepan over medium heat, and then add to the biscuit crumbs and pulse until well blended and starting to clump. Pour the mixture into the center of the prepared springform pan. Press the mixture firmly over the base of the pan with your fingers or with the bottom of a glass. Transfer the base to the fridge to chill for about 30 minutes, until firm.

To make the white chocolate cheesecake, melt the white chocolate in a bowl over a pan of simmering water, ensuring the bottom of the bowl does not come into contact with the water. Allow to cool slightly. In the bowl of an electric stand mixer fitted with the whisk attachment, lightly whip the cream on medium speed until soft peaks form. Set aside. Using the electric stand mixer fitted with the paddle attachment, beat the cream cheese, granulated sugar, confectioners' sugar and vanilla bean paste on medium speed until smooth. With the mixer on low speed, pour in the melted white chocolate and mix until combined. Add the whipped cream and fold through. Pour the cheesecake mixture over the biscuit base into the springform pan and smooth the top with an offset spatula. Wrap in plastic wrap and chill the cheesecake in the fridge until completely set, for 6 hours minimum (preferably overnight).

To make the raspberry sauce, in a small saucepan, whisk together the sugar, cornstarch and lemon juice. Add the raspberries and over medium-low heat, bring the mixture to a boil, stirring constantly. Use the back of a spoon to squash the raspberries and break them down to a pulp. Simmer for 5 minutes, and then remove from the heat. Pass the raspberry sauce through a fine-mesh sieve, discarding the seeds. Set aside to cool completely.

When ready to serve, run a sharp knife between the edge of the cheesecake and springform pan all the way around, and then release the cheesecake. Pour half of the raspberry sauce over the cheesecake, and use an offset spatula to smear the sauce to the edges. Then decorate with raspberries, strawberries and red currants. Slice and serve with an extra drizzle of raspberry sauce, if desired. This can be stored covered in plastic wrap in the fridge for up to 5 days.

SHOWSTOPPER BLACK FOREST LAYER CAKE

Yield: **1** *(8-inch [20-cm]) 3-layer cake (12-14 slices)*

Lo and behold my showstopper for this chapter. A decadent three-layer chocolate cake layered with kirsch-soaked cherries and freshly whipped cream. Luxuriously topped with a thick layer of chocolate ganache, fresh cherries and chocolate curls, this cake will certainly be eye-catching. This is a bit of a retro gem that certainly earns its spot on the classic cake stage.

For the Chocolate Sponge

1 cup (230 g) unsalted butter, room temperature

½ cup (100 g) granulated sugar

½ cup (110 g) firmly packed brown sugar

4 large eggs, room temperature

1⅓ cups (200 g) 70% dark chocolate

1¾ cups (220 g) all-purpose flour

¾ cup (70 g) unsweetened cocoa powder

2 tsp (9 g) baking powder

1 tsp baking soda

½ tsp salt

1 cup (240 ml) buttermilk, room temperature

2 tsp (10 ml) vanilla extract

For the Cherry Syrup

1 (14½-oz [411-g]) can pitted black cherries in syrup

2 tbsp (30 g) granulated sugar

2 tsp (5 g) cornstarch

3 tbsp (45 ml) kirsch (cherry liquor)

For the Whipped Cream

1½ cups (360 ml) heavy cream, cold

6 tbsp (50 g) sifted confectioners' sugar

1½ tsp (7 ml) vanilla extract

Preheat the oven to 350°F (180°C). Grease the bases and sides of three 8-inch (20-cm) cake pans, and line the bases with parchment paper.

To make the chocolate sponge cakes, in the bowl of an electric stand mixer fitted with the paddle attachment, cream the butter, granulated sugar and brown sugar on medium speed for 5 minutes, or until pale. Reduce the speed to low, and add the eggs one at a time, beating well after each addition until well incorporated. Ensure that you scrape down the sides of the bowl. Melt the chocolate in a bowl set over a pan of simmering water, ensuring the bottom of the bowl does not come into contact with the water. Beating continuously, slowly pour the melted chocolate into the mixer bowl, and beat until combined.

In a separate bowl sift the flour, cocoa powder, baking powder, baking soda and salt and mix. Fold the dry ingredients into the wet ingredients until evenly incorporated, and then mix in the buttermilk and vanilla until smooth. Divide the batter evenly between the three prepared cake pans, and smooth out with an offset spatula. Bake for 20 to 25 minutes, or until the center springs back after being pressed gently or a toothpick inserted comes out clean. Cool in the pans for a few minutes, and then remove from the pans, peel off the parchment and cool on a wire rack. If the sponge layers have domed, level them off with a serrated knife.

While the cakes are baking, make the cherry syrup. Drain the pitted black cherries, reserving the cherry juice, and place the cherries from the can into a bowl and set aside. Add the sugar and cornstarch into a saucepan and stir together. While continuously stirring, pour in ½ cup (120 ml) of the reserved cherry juice. (You can discard the leftover cherry juice.) Add the kirsch and place the saucepan over medium heat. Bring the mixture to a boil, stirring continuously, and simmer until thickened (this doesn't take long). Stir in the cherries until combined and set aside to cool completely.

To prepare the cream, in the bowl of an electric stand mixer fitted with the whisk attachment, add the cream, confectioners' sugar and vanilla, and on medium speed, whip until soft peaks have formed. Refrigerate until needed.

For the Chocolate Ganache
¾ cup (180 ml) heavy cream
⅔ cup (100 g) finely chopped
70% dark chocolate

For Assembling
⅔ cup (220 g) black cherry jam,
store-bought
2 cups (275 g) fresh cherries
Chocolate curls (optional)

Tip: To make chocolate curls, melt ⅓ cup (50 g) of coarsely chopped 70% dark chocolate in a bowl set over a pan of simmering water, ensuring the bottom of the bowl does not come into contact with the water. Once melted, spread the chocolate on a clean baking sheet, in a thin layer. Put the cookie sheet in the fridge to set for 1 hour. Remove from the fridge, and then scrape carefully using a long, sharp knife held at a slight angle, until the chocolate curls up towards you. If the chocolate feels too hard to create the curls, allow the cookie sheet to sit at room temperature for the chocolate to warm a little before trying again. Once the curls are created, put them back in the fridge until needed.

To make the chocolate ganache, in a small saucepan over medium heat, heat the cream until hot and simmering at the edges, but do not allow it to boil. Place the chopped chocolate in a bowl, pour the hot cream over the chocolate and leave to stand for 5 minutes. Then stir until the chocolate has fully melted and is smooth. Leave to cool to room temperature.

To assemble, place one of the cakes onto a serving plate and spread over half of the cherry jam, smoothing to the edge. Dollop half of the whipped cream onto the jam, and using an offset spatula or the back of a spoon, smooth it out evenly. Spoon half of the kirsch cherries onto the whipped cream. Place the second layer of sponge on top of the cherries and repeat the process with the remaining jam, whipped cream and kirsch cherries. Top with the last chocolate sponge layer. Spread the chocolate ganache onto the top of the final sponge layer. Decorate with fresh cherries and chocolate curls (if desired). Leftovers can be stored wrapped in plastic wrap in the fridge for up to 3 days.

PUDDINGS TO GIVE YOU THE WARM FUZZIES

My love for old-fashioned puddings was formed early on in my life during my English boarding school days. As is standard in most English schools, our meals were finished off with a pudding, particularly in the colder months. It was here that I fell hard for all things custard-based, warm sponges and steaming bowls of jammy rice pudding.

In the UK, the term "pudding" encapsulates any type of homey, rustic dessert traditionally made out of pantry staples and, more often than not, served with custard or a sauce. These types of desserts provide the perfect warm, comforting and cozy vibes when the coldness outside surrounds our homes. Enjoying a large square of my School Days Chocolate Malt Sponge with Chocolate Custard (page 99) takes me right back to the 1980s. Steamed Orange Treacle Sponge Pudding (page 101), Sticky Ginger Date Pudding (page 112) and Chocolate Peanut Butter Molten Lava Cakes (page 115) are other classics to which I've given delicious, inviting twists.

But I don't want you to think that puddings are only for the winter months. British Black Currant and Plum Queen of Puddings (page 108), which has to be the prettiest of them all, Summer Grilled Peach and Mint Eton Mess (page 111) and Stone Fruit Coconut Crumble (page 116) are perfect for summer. Get that sun hat on, grab an ice-cold bevvy and feel the sun's warmth on your back as you enjoy these light, fruit-filled desserts. Whatever time of year, you'll find a pudding to suit!

SCHOOL DAYS CHOCOLATE MALT SPONGE WITH CHOCOLATE CUSTARD

Yield: 1 *(9-inch [23-cm]) square sponge cake (12-16 servings)*

Sitting in the lunchroom, squashed together like sardines on a bench with a bowl of light chocolate sponge doused in steaming chocolate custard . . . this dessert brings me right back to those school days and the enjoyment I had in eating it. This treat is by far my favorite from my years in boarding school! My version adds malt powder and Maltesers® to the fluffy chocolate sponge, which imparts a nutty, toasty flavor full of nostalgia. The rich chocolate custard is a non-negotiable addition to this school dinner pudding. For extra fun, I've crumbled Maltesers on top for additional crunch and malt flavor.

For the Malt Chocolate Sponge

1 cup (230 g) unsalted butter, room temperature, plus more for greasing baking pan

¾ cup (150 g) granulated sugar

½ cup (110 g) firmly packed light brown sugar

4 large eggs, room temperature

1 tsp vanilla extract

1¾ cups (220 g) self-rising flour

½ cup (45 g) unsweetened cocoa powder

1 tsp baking powder

¼ tsp salt

¼ cup (45 g) malt powder

¼ cup (60 ml) milk

1 cup (90 g) Maltesers, plus 1 cup (90 g) to serve

Preheat the oven to 350°F (180°C). Grease a 9 x 9–inch (23 x 23–cm) baking pan with butter and line with parchment paper.

To make the chocolate sponge, in the bowl of an electric stand mixer, fitted with the paddle attachment, beat the butter, granulated sugar and light brown sugar for about 5 minutes, or until light and creamy. Add the eggs one at a time, beating until combined between each addition. Add the vanilla. Ensure that you scrape down the sides of the bowl. In a separate bowl, sift the flour, cocoa powder, baking powder, salt and malt powder. Stir to combine. Add half the dry ingredients to the batter and mix on low until just combined. Then add the milk and mix again until just incorporated. Finally, add the remaining dry ingredients and Maltesers, and fold through with a rubber spatula, until only a couple of streaks remain.

Pour the batter into the prepared pan and level with an offset spatula. Bake for 35 to 40 minutes, or until the center of the sponge springs back up if gently pressed and an inserted toothpick comes out clean. Remove the pan from the oven, and cool the sponge in the pan for 10 minutes before turning out onto a wire rack to cool completely.

(continued)

For the Chocolate Custard

1 cup (240 ml) milk

1 cup (240 ml) heavy cream

3 large egg yolks, room temperature

¼ cup (50 g) granulated sugar

1 tbsp (5 g) unsweetened cocoa powder

1 tbsp (8 g) cornstarch

¼ tsp salt

1 cup (150 g) finely chopped 70% dark chocolate

Tip: If you are unable to find Maltesers, then Whoppers are a good alternative.

While the sponge is baking, make the chocolate custard. In a saucepan over medium heat, heat the milk and cream together until just simmering and bubbles appear around the edge, but not boiling. Remove from the heat. In a large bowl placed on a tea towel (to prevent it from slipping), add the egg yolks, sugar, cocoa powder, cornstarch and salt, and whisk until pale and combined. While continuously whisking the egg mixture, slowly pour one-quarter of the milk and cream mixture in a thin steady stream into the egg mixture to temper it. Then gradually add the remaining milk and cream, whisking until well combined.

Pour the custard mixture back into the saucepan, add the chopped chocolate and cook on medium-low heat, whisking constantly, until the chocolate has melted and the mixture forms into a thick and smooth custard that thickly coats the back of a wooden spoon. Ensure that it doesn't boil, otherwise the custard will curdle. Strain the custard through a sieve set over a medium bowl to ensure that there aren't any lumps, and pour into a serving dish. Cut the sponge into squares while they are still warm and serve with the hot custard and crumbled Maltesers. This can be stored at room temperature in an airtight container for up to 3 days or in the refrigerator for up to 5 days.

STEAMED ORANGE TREACLE SPONGE PUDDING

Yield: **8–10** *servings*

Steamed puddings are deemed an old-fashioned dessert, but I find them totally underrated.
By using this method of cooking, you're left with sponge that is so light, moist and sticky,
having soaked up all the treacle goodness. This is comfort food taken to the next level and
is best served liberally with steaming hot vanilla custard.

⅔ cup (150 g) unsalted butter, room temperature, plus more for greasing basin

1 orange, rinsed and thinly sliced

½ cup (120 ml) golden syrup, plus 3 tbsp (45 ml) to serve

¾ cup (150 g) granulated sugar

Zest of 1 large orange

3 large eggs, room temperature

1¼ cups (155 g) self-rising flour

1 tsp baking powder

¼ tsp salt

3 tbsp (45 ml) whole milk

Hot vanilla custard, to serve

Grease a 1-quart (1-L) heatproof pudding basin with butter, and arrange the orange slices on the base and around the sides. Pour the golden syrup over the orange slices.

In a small bowl, combine the sugar and orange zest, and using your fingertips, rub the two together for 1 minute to release the oils of the zest into the sugar. In the bowl of an electric stand mixer fitted with the paddle attachment, cream the butter and sugar and zest mixture together on medium speed for 5 minutes, or until pale. Reduce the speed to low, and add the eggs one at a time, beating well after each addition until well incorporated. Ensure that you scrape down the sides of the bowl.

In a separate bowl sift the flour, baking powder and salt, and mix. Gently fold the dry ingredients into the cake batter until evenly incorporated, and then carefully mix in the milk until the batter is smooth. Pour the batter into the pudding basin and smooth the top of the batter.

(continued)

Tear a piece of parchment paper and aluminum foil, large enough to cover the top of the bowl and go halfway down either side, and place the foil on top of the parchment. Make sure to create a pleat down the center so that the sponge will have space to rise while cooking. Place the foil and parchment paper over the top of the bowl and tie a string tightly around the rim of the bowl. Trim any excess paper and foil, leaving a ¼-inch (6-mm) border under the string. Place an upturned heatproof saucer, small plate or trivet into a large, deep saucepan and sit the pudding on top. Add boiling water until it comes halfway up the basin but doesn't touch the parchment paper. Cover the pan with a tight-fitting lid and place over low heat. Allow to steam in the gently simmering water for 1¾ to 2 hours, adding more water to the pan if necessary. Make sure the pan does not boil dry. The sponge is ready when a skewer inserted into the center comes out clean. Carefully remove the pudding from the pan.

Cut the string from the basin and discard the foil and paper. Run a flat-bladed knife around the edge of the pudding to loosen the sides, carefully invert onto a serving plate with a rim and remove the basin. Pour the extra golden syrup over the top of the hot pudding and serve with hot custard. This can be stored tightly covered in plastic wrap in the refrigerator for up to 4 days.

Tips: A pudding basin refers to a ceramic or heatproof glass bowl that can be steamed. Often these types of bowls are used as mixing bowls.

The orange slices really do need to be sliced as thinly as you can so that they soften enough when cooked. If you struggle to do this, I suggest removing the rind before slicing.

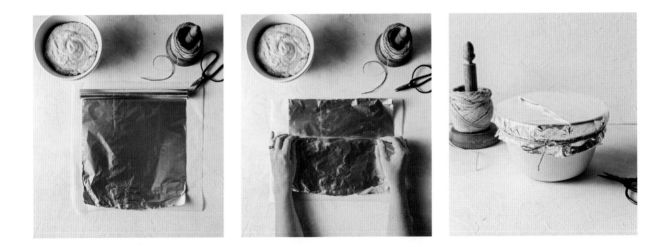

BLACKBERRY AND FIG BREAD AND BUTTER PUDDING

Yield: **8–10** *servings*

Here we have another British institution of the boarding school food scene—and one which I truly loved. Traditionally made with stale bread and raisins, I've turned this classic pudding on its head by using rich, buttery brioche soaked in delicious vanilla custard and dotted with blackberries and figs. This really is a pudding lover's dream.

Butter, for greasing baking dish

1 loaf (400 g) brioche bread, cut into ½" (1.3-cm)-thick slices

2 cups (280 g) fresh or frozen blackberries, halved if large, plus extra to serve (optional)

1¼ cups (300 ml) whole milk

½ cup (120 ml) heavy cream

3 large eggs, room temperature

¼ cup (50 g) granulated sugar

1 tsp vanilla extract

½ tsp salt

3 figs, quartered, plus extra to serve (optional)

2 tbsp (30 ml) maple syrup

Boiling water, as needed

¼ cup (30 g) slivered almonds

1 tsp confectioners' sugar, to dust

Grease an 8 x 10–inch (20 x 25–cm) baking dish with butter. Later on, this baking dish will need to sit inside a roasting pan with high sides.

Cut the brioche slices into triangles. Layer two to three slices flat in the bottom of the baking dish. Scatter half the blackberries over this bottom layer. Layer overlapping triangles of the remaining brioche on top of this base layer and sprinkle with the remaining blackberries.

To make the custard, in a large mixing bowl, whisk together the milk, cream, eggs, granulated sugar, vanilla and salt. Pour the custard all over the brioche in the dish, and gently press the exposed bread crusts down into the liquid to soak, although some of the brioche will stick up above the level of the custard mixture. Leave to stand for 20 minutes to allow the bread to soak up the custard.

While the pudding is resting, preheat the oven to 350°F (180°C).

In a small bowl, toss the figs and maple syrup together until coated, and set aside. Sit the baking dish inside a roasting pan with high sides. Add enough boiling water to come about halfway up the outside of the baking dish. (You can cook the pudding without the water bath, but this method ensures a lovely velvety texture.) Bake for 20 minutes covered in aluminum foil. Remove the foil and nestle the maple-coated figs in between the brioche slices, and then scatter the almonds on top. Bake for 15 to 20 minutes, or until just set in the middle. Remove from the oven and dust with the confectioners' sugar. Serve warm with fresh blackberries and figs, if using. This can be stored in the refrigerator tightly wrapped in plastic wrap for up to 4 days.

Tip: A 9-inch (23-cm) square baking pan or a 9-inch (23-cm) round pie pan can be used instead.

COCONUT RICE PUDDING WITH CARAMELIZED PINEAPPLE

Yield: **5–6 servings**

Having spent a large part of my childhood living as an expatriate in Asia, I was lucky enough to spend holidays in some far-flung places such as Thailand. I adore Thai food for the lightness and fragrance that's imparted in its cuisine. Here I've used beautiful-tasting lemongrass, kaffir lime and coconut milk, which are integral components of Thai cooking. They give this rice pudding a fresh twist on its more classic and familiar rendition. If I shut my eyes, I'm transported to the white sandy beach in Phuket with the warm waters lapping at my feet.

For the Coconut Rice Pudding

1 (14-oz [403-ml]) can unsweetened coconut milk, room temperature, divided

2 tbsp (30 g) unsalted butter

¼ cup (50 g) granulated sugar

1 cup (200 g) uncooked arborio rice

3 cups (720 ml) whole milk

1 lemongrass stalk, bruised

2 kaffir lime leaves, fresh or dried

1 tsp vanilla bean paste or extract

½ cup (30 g) coconut flakes

For the Caramelized Pineapple

½ cup (100 g) granulated sugar

¼ cup (60 g) unsalted butter

½ fresh pineapple, cored, sliced and quartered (or 4 canned pineapple rings, cut in quarters)

½ tsp ground ginger

2 kaffir lime leaves, stem removed and finely shredded (optional)

To make the coconut rice pudding, stir the coconut milk in its can. Pour out ½ cup (120 ml), and set it aside to be used in the caramelized pineapple. Melt the butter in a large, heavy-based saucepan over medium-low heat. Add the sugar and stir until dissolved. Add the rice, stirring to coat. Cook until the rice has swelled slightly, about 5 minutes. Pour in the coconut milk from the can, milk, lemongrass and kaffir lime leaves. Over a medium heat, bring the mixture to a boil, and then turn down to a simmer. Gently cook for 35 to 40 minutes, stirring frequently so that the rice doesn't stick to the bottom, until the rice pudding has thickened. Turn the heat off when the rice pudding still looks a bit runny, as it will carry on soaking up the liquid as it cools. Stir in the vanilla.

While the rice pudding is cooking, in a medium-sized frying pan, toast the coconut flakes over medium heat, stirring constantly, until fragrant and golden, about 4 minutes. Transfer to a plate to cool.

To make the caramelized pineapple, place the sugar in a medium-sized frying pan over low heat and without stirring, allow the sugar to dissolve and turn a golden amber color. Add the remaining coconut milk you had set aside; it will froth, so whisk hard until incorporated and allow the mixture to bubble for 5 minutes. Add the butter, and whisk continuously until it melts. Add the pineapple and ginger, and cook for 4 to 5 minutes, stirring occasionally.

Once ready to serve, remove the lemongrass stalk and kaffir lime leaves from the rice and scoop the rice pudding into bowls while it is still hot. Spoon the pineapple over the pudding and drizzle with any remaining caramel sauce from the pineapples. Sprinkle with flaked coconut and shredded kaffir lime leaves (if using). This can be kept in the refrigerator in an airtight container for up to 4 days.

Tips: If you are unable to find kaffir lime leaves, don't worry. The rice pudding will still taste lovely and fragrant without them.

Add 1 tablespoon (15 ml) of rum to the caramelized pineapple for a little kick!

Yield: **8–10** *servings*

As a nation, we Brits love pudding, probably because pudding tends to be better suited to the colder autumn and winter months when hearty desserts are wanted. However, this Queen of Puddings is perfect for the warmer months, with its light custard pudding base, bright black currant jam and sliced plums and meringue peaks on top. This delicious old-fashioned pudding may stem from humble beginnings of cupboard staples, but it really is a thing of beauty fit for a queen.

For the Pudding Base

2 tbsp (30 g) unsalted butter, softened, plus extra for greasing

2½ cups (600 ml) whole milk

Zest of 1 large lemon

¼ tsp of salt

4 large egg yolks

¼ cup (50 g) granulated sugar

1 tsp vanilla extract

1½ cups (150 g) slightly stale white breadcrumbs

For the Jammy Fruit

1 tbsp (8 g) cornstarch

2 tsp (10 ml) fresh lemon juice

⅔ cup (220 g) black currant jam or conserve

2 cups (320 g) pitted and sliced plums (about 4 plums)

For the Meringue

4 large egg whites

1 cup (200 g) superfine caster sugar

Tip: Traditionally the meringue in Queen of Puddings has a soft and marshmallowy interior and a barely golden-kissed exterior. If you would like a crispier outside, use a kitchen blowtorch after baking to scorch the meringue.

To make the pudding base, preheat the oven to 350°F (180°C) and grease an 8 x 10–inch (20 x 25–cm) shallow oval or rectangular baking dish (one that will fit into a roasting pan) with butter.

In a saucepan over medium heat, gently warm the milk, butter, lemon zest and salt, until the butter has melted, but don't let it boil. In a large bowl, lightly whisk the egg yolks, sugar and vanilla until combined. Slowly pour the warm milk into the eggs, whisking continuously. Add the breadcrumbs and stir until fully combined. Pour the mixture into the greased baking dish, and leave it to stand for 15 minutes. Carefully transfer the dish to a roasting pan and fill the pan with boiling water about halfway up the sides of the baking dish. Bake the custard for 20 to 25 minutes, or until the custard has set but is still a bit wobbly in the middle. Remove the roasting pan from the oven and carefully lift out the baking dish. Set the dish aside to cool while you make the jam and meringue.

To make the jammy fruit, in a small saucepan over low heat, combine the cornstarch and lemon juice and whisk to make a slurry. Add the jam and plums and warm gently for 10 minutes, or until the plums start to soften. Set aside.

To make the meringue, in a clean bowl of an electric stand mixer fitted with the whisk attachment, place the egg whites and whisk on medium-high speed until stiff peaks form. Whisk in the caster sugar, 1 tablespoon (13 g) at a time, and continue to whisk for 5 minutes to form a thick, glossy meringue. Transfer the meringue mixture to a piping bag fitted with an open star tip nozzle. Once the pudding base has cooled slightly, carefully spread the jam and plum slices on top. Then pipe the meringue over the jam layer. Alternatively, dollop the meringue onto the jam layer, and using the back of a spoon, swirl it around.

Lower the oven temperature to 300°F (150°C). Return the baking dish to the oven (not in the roasting tray this time) and bake for 25 to 30 minutes, or until the meringue is bronzed and crisp on top. Let the pudding stand for 15 minutes before serving. This can be stored in the refrigerator lightly wrapped in plastic wrap for 3 to 4 days.

SUMMER GRILLED PEACH AND MINT ETON MESS

Yield: 6-8 servings

The classic combination of crisp broken-up meringue, dollops of whipped cream and fresh fruit has become a bit of an English institution in the summertime. This universally loved dessert is given a vibrant twist with the addition of fresh mint in the whipped cream and crème fraîche, and resting the grilled peaches atop a dollop of sweet-yet-tangy lemon curd brings out their juices and intensifies their flavor. All the components can be made ahead of time, making this an easy-to-assemble dessert for any occasion.

For the Meringue

3 large egg whites

¾ cup (150 g) granulated sugar

1 tsp fresh lemon juice

1 tsp cornstarch

For the Whipped Mint Cream

1¼ cups (300 ml) heavy cream

½ cup (120 ml) crème fraîche

⅓ cup (40 g) sifted confectioners' sugar

1 tsp vanilla bean paste

2 tbsp (11 g) fresh mint leaves

For the Grilled Peaches and Serving

2 tbsp (30 g) unsalted butter

2 cups (345 g) halved, pitted and sliced ripe peaches (about 3 large peaches)

2 tbsp (30 g) firmly packed brown sugar

½ cup (120 ml) lemon curd, store-bought

Tip: Alternatively, layer the meringue, cream, lemon curd and peaches into a glass, and repeat the layering until you reach the top of the glass.

Preheat the oven to 275°F (135°C). Line a baking sheet with parchment paper.

To make the meringue, place the egg whites in the bowl of a stand mixer fitted with the whisk attachment, and whisk on medium speed until soft peaks form when the whisk is removed, about 5 minutes. While whisking, gradually add the sugar one spoonful at a time, whisking well between each spoonful. Once all the sugar is added, whisk in the lemon juice and cornstarch, and continue to whisk for another 5 minutes. By now, the mixture should be thick and glossy, and the sugar should be fully incorporated. If you rub a bit of mixture between your thumb and finger, there should be no grit as the sugar should be fully blended. If there is still some grit, continue whipping for a couple more minutes. Scoop the meringue mixture onto the baking sheet, and spread the meringue into a thin layer with a spatula into an approximately 8 x 12–inch (20 x 30–cm) rectangle. Turn the oven temperature down to 225°F (110°C). Bake the meringue for 60 minutes, and then turn off the oven, keeping the oven door closed. Let the meringue cool for about 1 hour, or until the oven is cool.

While the meringue is cooling, prepare the whipped mint cream. In a large bowl, add the cream, crème fraîche, confectioners' sugar and vanilla, and whisk until soft peaks form. Slice the mint leaves thinly and fold into the whipped cream. Refrigerate the cream until ready to serve.

To grill the peaches, melt the butter in a small saucepan over low heat. Place a large skillet on medium-high heat. In a medium bowl, add the peaches with the melted butter and brown sugar and mix to coat. Place the peaches on their side on the hot skillet, and grill for 3 minutes. Flip over and grill for 3 to 5 minutes, or until browned and tender.

To serve, once all the peach slices have been grilled, remove the mint cream from the fridge. Break up the meringue slab into roughly 2-inch (5-cm) pieces. In a bowl or on a plate, add some meringue pieces, dollop a spoonful of mint cream onto the meringue and follow up with a spoonful of lemon curd. Add two to three slices of grilled peaches and some extra mint leaves. Any leftovers can be stored in separate airtight containers in the fridge for up to 3 days.

STICKY GINGER DATE PUDDING

Yield: 1 (9-inch [23-cm]) square sponge cake (12–16 servings)

Sticky date pudding brings me back to my university days. My mates and I would pile into a car and head to The Trout Inn on the outskirts of Oxford for a hearty weekend pub meal. This beautiful, 17th-century pub sits on the banks of the River Thames and served the best desserts, one of which was sticky toffee pudding with vanilla ice cream. I've added chopped dates and two types of ginger to my version to add even more warmth and substance to this light, moist sponge cake. And just like in the pub, this is best served hot with a generous pour of sweet toffee sauce and a scoop of ice cream.

For the Ginger Date Sponge

½ cup (115 g) unsalted butter, room temperature, plus more for greasing

1½ cups (260 g) finely chopped pitted dates

1¼ cups (300 ml) boiling water

1 tsp baking soda

¾ cup (165 g) firmly packed brown sugar

3 large eggs, room temperature

1 tsp pure vanilla extract

5 balls (80 g) stem ginger, drained and finely chopped

1¾ cups (220 g) self-rising flour

2 tsp (8 g) ground ginger

For the Toffee Sauce

⅔ cup (135 g) loosely packed brown sugar

1¼ cups (300 ml) heavy cream

⅓ cup (75 g) unsalted butter

2 tbsp (30 ml) golden syrup

For Serving

Cream or vanilla ice cream

Preheat the oven to 350°F (180°C). Grease a 9 x 9–inch (23 x 23–cm) baking pan with butter. Line with parchment paper, allowing it to hang over the sides of the pan to create a sling.

To make the ginger date sponge, in a medium bowl, combine the dates, boiling water and baking soda and cover with a plate. Let it stand for 15 minutes. Mash the dates with a fork. In the bowl of an electric stand mixer fitted with the paddle attachment, cream the butter and brown sugar on medium speed until pale and fluffy. Scrape down the sides of the bowl. Add the eggs one at a time, beating well after each addition. Add the vanilla, date mixture and stem ginger and fold together. The batter may split, but it will come together when you add the flour. Sift the flour into a medium bowl, add the ground ginger and give it a quick stir. Add the flour mixture to the batter and fold until just combined. Pour the batter into the prepared pan. Bake for 40 to 45 minutes, or until the cake is browned on top or the center springs back when gently pressed and an inserted toothpick comes out clean. Let the cake cool for 10 minutes in the pan before serving.

While the sponge is cooking, make the toffee sauce. In a medium saucepan over medium heat, combine the brown sugar, cream, butter and golden syrup. Heat, stirring occasionally, until the butter and sugar have melted and bubbles appear in the center. Continue cooking at a low simmer for about 5 minutes, or until the sauce has thickened and coats the back of a spoon. Remove from the heat and pour into a pitcher or measuring cup.

Using the parchment paper, lift the sponge from the pan and place onto a serving plate. Slice into 16 squares and serve warm with toffee sauce and cream or vanilla ice cream. This can be stored in an airtight container for up to 3 days in the refrigerator.

Tip: For an extra-soft, moist sponge, once you remove the cake from the oven, poke holes all over, and pour half of the toffee sauce over the top, allowing it to seep into all the holes for 15 minutes before serving.

CHOCOLATE PEANUT BUTTER MOLTEN LAVA CAKES

Yield: **6 servings**

These individual chocolate puddings are irresistible, to say the least. During my year backpacking straight after university, I lived in Port Douglas in Tropical North Queensland for a couple of months working as a waitress. I served this delicious treat multiple times a night and was always happy after service when the chef treated me to a leftover pudding! The outside layer of the sponge is cooked, yet the inside remains gooey with a decadent melting peanut butter center. Chocolate and peanut butter are truly a match made in heaven. These cakes are surprisingly quick to make, and you'll be sure to wow your guests when they break open the sponge to reveal the mouthwatering interior.

½ cup (115 g) unsalted butter, room temperature, plus extra for buttering the molds

Cocoa powder, for dusting

1 cup (150 g) finely chopped 70% dark chocolate

2 large eggs, room temperature

2 egg yolks, room temperature

¾ cup (165 g) firmly packed light brown sugar

½ cup (65 g) sifted all-purpose flour

¼ tsp salt

½ cup (130 g) smooth peanut butter

Heavy cream, to serve

Preheat the oven to 400°F (200°C). Generously butter six 6-ounce (180-ml) ceramic ramekins, and dust them with cocoa powder, knocking any excess out. Place the ramekins on a baking sheet and set aside until needed.

Melt the chocolate and butter in a bowl set over a pan of simmering water, ensuring the bottom of the bowl does not come into contact with the water. Stir until combined. Remove from the heat and allow to cool slightly. Alternatively, melt in a microwave in 15-second bursts.

In the bowl of an electric stand mixer fitted with the paddle attachment, beat the eggs, the egg yolks and sugar on medium speed for 5 minutes, or until thickened and pale. Fold in the melted chocolate, flour and salt.

Spoon two-thirds of the mixture equally between the ramekins. Then divide the peanut butter into the center of each ramekin and spoon the remaining chocolate mixture on top. Bake for 12 to 13 minutes, or until just set on the outside but the centers still have a wobble. Remove from the oven and let the cakes stand in the ramekins for 1 minute. Gently run a knife around the edges of the cakes to loosen. Invert the ramekins onto a dessert plate, and let them sit for 10 seconds or so. Tap the top of the ramekin with a spoon to loosen the cake, gently remove the ramekin to reveal the cake underneath, dust with cocoa powder and then top with cream to serve. These can be stored in the refrigerator wrapped tightly in plastic wrap for up to 3 days, but they will lose that gooey consistency in the center.

Notes: Each oven is different, and whether you use metal dariole molds or ceramic ramekins will alter the cook time. Cook times can vary between 9 to 13 minutes. I suggest testing one lava cake to get the perfect timing that suits your oven.

Alternative fillings to peanut butter can be caramel sauce, chocolate hazelnut spread or jam.

STONE FRUIT COCONUT CRUMBLE

Yield: **10-12** *servings*

This gorgeous recipe is a much-loved family favorite. Fruit crumble is one of the most versatile desserts; a variety or any combination of fruit will work brilliantly, making this a year-round seasonal pudding. Here, I've used a selection of beautiful summer stone fruit like peaches, nectarines and apricots and teamed them alongside a tasty coconut crumble. This crumble is the perfect way to end a meal.

For the Fruit Filling

4 cups (1 kg) mixed stone fruit (about 4 peaches, 4 nectarines and 4 apricots)

½ cup (110 g) firmly packed light brown sugar

½ tsp salt

3 tbsp (45 ml) fresh orange juice

Zest of 1 large orange

2 tbsp (16 g) cornstarch

2 tsp (10 ml) vanilla extract

For the Crumble Topping

¾ cup (100 g) all-purpose flour

⅓ cup (65 g) granulated sugar

½ cup (50 g) shredded coconut

½ cup (45 g) rolled oats

⅔ cup (150 g) unsalted butter, roughly chopped

½ cup (55 g) slivered almonds

¼ cup (20 g) coconut flakes, toasted

Preheat the oven to 350°F (180°C).

To make the fruit filling, halve and pit the fruit and cut it into thin wedges. In a medium saucepan over medium heat, combine the fruit, brown sugar, salt, orange juice and zest. Cook for 5 to 10 minutes, or until the fruit softens but is still holding its shape, stirring often. If your stone fruit is soft, juicy and very ripe, you don't need to heat it in the saucepan. Instead, add all the fruit filling ingredients into a large mixing bowl, and mix before transferring to the baking pan. Remove the saucepan from the heat. Stir in the cornstarch and vanilla. Transfer to a round 9-inch (23-cm) baking pan.

To make the crumble topping, in a large bowl, mix together the flour, sugar, shredded coconut and oats. Add the butter, and rub the mixture and butter together with your fingers until you have a soft, crumbly topping that resembles fine breadcrumbs. Add the almonds and mix together with your hands. Squeeze some of the crumble together to make small clumps.

Heap the crumble topping over the fruit, and place the baking dish onto a baking sheet to catch any juices that might escape during cooking. Bake for 30 minutes, or until golden brown on top. Remove from the oven and sprinkle with toasted coconut flakes. This can be stored covered in plastic wrap in the refrigerator for up to 4 days and reheated in the oven.

Tip: Omit the shredded and flaked coconut for a more traditional fruit crumble.

DOWN·MEMORY·LANE SNACKS
AND SWEET PASTRIES

Aren't food memories amazing? That connection through taste, smell or feeling that brings you back to a different time or place can always make you smile. In this chapter filled with snacks and sweet pastries, I want you too to be transported back in time. From the fudge you ate at your grandma's house, to the brioche scrolls you enjoyed from your favorite bakery years ago, there are many sweet treats in this chapter that will no doubt bring out the nostalgia in you.

The chapter starts off with delicious small bites such as Grandpa's Chocolate Amaretto Truffles (page 121), Chocolate Swirl Vanilla Bean Marshmallows (page 123), and White Chocolate Gingerbread Fudge (page 127). All of these are fantastic ideas for gifts—wrapped in a cellophane bag and tied with a ribbon, they'll delight any recipient.

I then move onto bigger snacks and treats that would be thoroughly enjoyed for afternoon tea, such as the Teatime Treat Spiced Plum and Hazelnut Friands (page 131) and Aussie Strawberry and Lemon Lamingtons (page 135). These two recipes evoke memories of my many years living in Australia. (I mean, you don't get more classic than a good ol' lamington. If you've never had one, it's a fun recipe to make, and the kids will love it!)

This chapter ends with two recipes using enriched dough—an excellent dough to have in your back pocket for making cinnamon rolls, babka, brioche rolls and even filled donuts. It's truly one of the most versatile doughs out there. I share with you Blackberry-Glazed Brioche Donuts (page 138) and Maple-Glazed Apple Pecan Scrolls (page 141) as two great examples of what to bake with brioche dough.

GRANDPA'S CHOCOLATE AMARETTO TRUFFLES

Yield: **24–28 truffles**

When we'd visit my grandparents in Northern England at Christmastime, it became a tradition that I'd make them chocolate truffles. My grandpa loved them, especially if they were spiked with booze! Making these always brings back super-fond memories, and with this recipe, you can roll the truffles in chopped nuts or use the advanced technique of tempering the chocolate for coating the truffles. Regardless of which way you choose, I hope you enjoy making them as much as I do and enjoy eating them as much as my grandpa did.

For the Truffle Filling

3 cups (450 g) finely chopped 70% dark chocolate

¾ cup (180 ml) heavy cream

1 tsp unsalted butter

3 tbsp (45 ml) amaretto

⅓ cup (35 g) slivered toasted almonds

To make the truffle filling, melt the dark chocolate in a bowl set over a pan of simmering water, ensuring the bottom of the bowl does not come into contact with the water. This should take about 5 minutes. Once the chocolate has melted, remove from the heat. In a small, heavy saucepan over medium-low heat, bring the cream to a simmer. Stir, scraping the sides with a spatula every few minutes to ensure even heat. Pour a small amount of cream into the chocolate, and stir until combined. Repeat another few times until all the cream has been added and combined with the chocolate. Add the butter and amaretto, and stir until the butter is melted and the chocolate is smooth. Cover the filling, allow to cool and then refrigerate for 2 hours, or until it's firm enough to shape.

Line two small baking sheets with parchment paper. Using a teaspoon or melon baller, measure out equal-sized amounts of filling. (If you want uniformity, measure out 1½ tablespoons [20 g] per scoop.) Gently roll each piece into a ball between your hands and place on the prepared baking sheets. Add the slivered almonds to a small bowl, and then individually roll half of the truffles into the chopped nuts and place onto one baking sheet. Refrigerate the second baking sheet with the remaining bare truffle balls for 30 minutes.

(continued)

For the Chocolate Coating

2 cups (300 g) finely chopped milk chocolate, divided

⅓ cup (50 g) finely chopped white chocolate

1 tsp natural flaked sea salt

To heat the chocolate for the chocolate coating, place 1⅓ cups (200 g) of the milk chocolate into a bowl over a saucepan of simmering water, ensuring that the base doesn't touch the chocolate. Use a rubber spatula to stir the chocolate until evenly melted. (Don't use a wooden spoon as it retains moisture and affects the chocolate.) Using a candy thermometer, keep an eye on the chocolate until it reaches 113°F (45°C), and remove the bowl from the heat. Add small amounts of the remaining unmelted milk chocolate, and stir in to melt. Continue adding small amounts of chocolate, stirring and melting until the chocolate temperature lowers to 80°F (27°C). (You may not use all the finely chopped chocolate.) Return the bowl over the saucepan, and bring the temperature back up until the chocolate reaches 84°F (29°C). The chocolate is now tempered and ready to use.

Remove the remaining bare truffle balls from the fridge and, one at a time, immerse the balls into the melted chocolate and use a fork to spin them around until fully coated. Lift each one out on the fork tines and tap the fork on the sides of the bowl so that the excess drips off and a thin chocolate shell forms around the truffle. Set the truffle onto the prepared baking sheet. Repeat with the remaining truffles. Refrigerate until the chocolate shells are set.

Melt the white chocolate in the microwave in 20-second increments, stirring the chocolate every so often until melted. Pour into a small piping bag and snip a small hole off the corner. Drizzle white chocolate over the milk chocolate–coated truffles. Sprinkle with sea salt, and refrigerate until set. Alternatively, once the truffle balls have been rolled, dip them into a bowl filled with cocoa powder for a cocoa dusting. Store the truffles in an airtight container for up to 2 weeks.

Tips: The temperatures stated in the tempering process are specific for milk chocolate and differ if using white or dark chocolate.

If the coating splits when the cream and chocolate are combined, add 1 tablespoon (15 ml) of boiling water to the ganache and whisk until it comes back together.

CHOCOLATE SWIRL VANILLA BEAN MARSHMALLOWS

Yield: **32 *marshmallows***

Marshmallows have to be one of the first sweets that we all fell in love with as children. Store-bought, white or pink, large or small, atop hot chocolate or in rocky road—that fluffy marshmallow and its powdery coating won us all over. But here's the thing: Homemade marshmallows are like nothing you've ever tasted. It's like biting down into a fluffy cloud. It literally melts away. I've added chocolate swirls throughout mine so that you get these wafer-thin layers of crunch that provide a divine textural sensation to the marshmallows.

For Prepping
1 tbsp (15 ml) vegetable oil for greasing, divided
½ cup (65 g) cornstarch
½ cup (60 g) confectioners' sugar

For the Gelatin
¾ cup (180 ml) water
1½ tbsp (45 g) gelatin powder

For the Sugar Syrup
3⅓ cups (665 g) granulated sugar
¼ cup plus 2 tbsp (90 ml) liquid glucose syrup
½ tsp salt
1⅛ cups (270 ml) water
3 large egg whites
1 tbsp (15 ml) vanilla bean paste

Lightly grease a deep-sided 9 x 13–inch (23 x 33–cm) baking dish with half of the vegetable oil. Line the dish with parchment paper and grease the paper with the remaining oil. Allow the parchment paper to hang over the sides to make it easier to lift the marshmallows out later. In a small bowl, add the cornstarch and confectioners' sugar and mix. Dust the baking dish with some of this mixture to coat the base and sides evenly. Reserve the remaining cornstarch and confectioners' sugar mixture for later.

To prepare the gelatin, place the water in a medium bowl. Add the gelatin powder, and mix to moisten the gelatin. Set aside to allow the gelatin to bloom while the sugar syrup is cooking (at least 10 minutes).

To make the sugar syrup, add the sugar, liquid glucose, salt and water to a deep, high-sided saucepan. Heat gently over medium-low heat, stirring until the sugar dissolves and it comes to a light boil. Stop stirring and add a candy thermometer. Turn the heat to high, and allow the syrup to continue to boil until it reaches 244°F (118°C). Add the gelatin, whisking all the time, being careful as it will bubble up. Whisk until the gelatin dissolves, and then remove from the heat and set aside.

Place the egg whites in the clean, grease-free bowl of an electric stand mixer fitted with the whisk attachment. Whisk on medium speed to soft peaks. Turn the mixer to low and pour the sugar syrup in a steady stream, down the side of the stand mixer bowl (not onto the whisk attachment) and into the egg whites. Add the vanilla bean paste, gradually increase the speed of the mixer until it's running on high and whip the marshmallow mixture for 10 minutes, until it has tripled in size and is stiff and shiny. You can tell it is done when you stop the mixer and lift up the beater and the marshmallow slowly drips back down into the bowl in a thick, shiny stream.

(continued)

¾ cup (115 g) finely chopped 70% dark chocolate

While the marshmallow mixer is beating, melt the dark chocolate in a heatproof bowl in the microwave in 20-second increments, stirring frequently until fully melted. Immediately spoon the melted chocolate over the top of the marshmallow mixture, and then very gently and slowly fold or swirl the chocolate into the marshmallow, making sure you don't overmix as that will result in loss of the swirl.

Pour the marshmallow mixture into the prepared dish and smooth the surface with an oiled spatula. Dust the top of the marshmallows with a little more of the confectioners' sugar and cornstarch mixture, and set aside in a cool, dry place for 6 hours minimum or overnight to set. (Don't chill in the fridge.)

Once the marshmallow mixture has set, turn out the marshmallow slab onto a clean countertop dusted with the remaining confectioners' sugar and cornstarch mixture. Peel off the parchment paper, and cut the marshmallow slab into cubes. Dredge the marshmallows in the confectioners' sugar and cornstarch mixture to coat. These can be stored in an airtight container at room temperature for up to 3 weeks.

Notes: It is best to measure out all of your ingredients and prepare the baking dish before starting. Also, oil your spatula so that the marshmallow mixture doesn't stick to it. A candy thermometer and stand mixer are essential pieces of equipment for this recipe.

Omit the melted chocolate for pure vanilla bean marshmallows. Or add in a couple of drops of peppermint extract along with the vanilla bean paste for a peppermint chocolate variation.

WHITE CHOCOLATE GINGERBREAD FUDGE

Yield: 32 fudge squares

Soft, crumbly, sweet fudge is a confection loved by all generations. Easy and quick to whip up, this makes a brilliant gift for family and friends, especially around Christmastime. My festive fudge pairs warming ginger with the sweet richness of white chocolate for a beautiful balance of flavors. The hardest part about making this is waiting for it to set!

¼ cup (60 g) unsalted butter, plus more for greasing

4 cups (600 g) finely chopped white chocolate

1 (14-oz [307-ml]) can condensed milk

1 tsp vanilla extract

¼ tsp salt

3 tbsp (45 ml) dark molasses

2 tsp (4 g) ground ginger

½ tsp ground cinnamon

Grease a 9 x 9–inch (23 x 23–cm) baking pan with butter and line with parchment paper. Allow the parchment paper to hang over the sides to make it easier to lift the fudge out once set.

In a medium saucepan over low heat, add the white chocolate and condensed milk together, stirring often until the chocolate is melted, smooth and combined. Add the butter, vanilla and salt, and stir constantly until melted and combined. Remove the pan from the heat. Pour half of the mixture into another small saucepan and set aside; this is your white chocolate fudge mixture. In the original saucepan, add the dark molasses, ginger and cinnamon, and stir until fully mixed in. This is your gingerbread fudge mixture.

To assemble your fudge, pour half of the white chocolate fudge into the prepared dish and spread out evenly with an offset spatula. Then, pour half of the gingerbread mixture over top and spread out. Repeat layering the white chocolate and gingerbread fudge until all of it has been used. If either of the fudges start to solidify at any point, place back onto the stovetop and gently warm through. Run a butter knife or a chopstick through the fudge to swirl and marble it slightly, making sure not to mix it too much.

Allow the fudge to cool to room temperature, then refrigerate for 4 hours or until completely firm. Cut with a hot knife into squares. Store your fudge in an airtight container in the fridge for up to 1 week.

DATE AND HONEY CRÈME FRAÎCHE SCONES

Yield: **8** *scones*

Traditional plain scones served with cream and jam are as quintessentially British as Wimbledon and cucumber sandwiches. A staple gracing any picnic blanket laid out for a cricket match or on a three-tiered cake stand at afternoon tea, flaky, buttery scones are a must. I've given these classics a makeover by adding chopped dates and honey into the dough before baking, which imparts little bursts of sweetness. Walnuts add pockets of crunch, and the crème fraîche creates a rich, light scone. Served with a dollop of thickened cream and an extra drizzle of honey, this simple recipe is a must-try.

2⅓ cups (290 g) self-rising flour, plus extra if needed

1½ tsp (7 g) baking powder

½ tsp salt

⅓ cup (75 g) unsalted butter, cold and cut into small cubes

Zest of 2 large oranges

⅔ cup (160 ml) crème fraîche, cold, plus extra if needed

1 large egg, beaten

3 tbsp (45 ml) honey, plus extra to serve

1 tsp vanilla bean paste

⅔ cup (115 g) pitted and chopped dates (small pieces)

½ cup (60 g) coarsely chopped toasted walnuts

1 tbsp (15 ml) milk, to brush over scones

Thickened cream and honey, to serve

Preheat the oven to 400°F (200°C). Line a baking sheet with parchment paper and set aside.

In a medium bowl, sift the flour, baking powder and salt. Add the butter and orange zest, and using your fingertips, rub the butter and flour together until the mixture resembles fine breadcrumbs with some larger pea-sized pieces. In a separate bowl add the crème fraîche, egg, honey and vanilla, and whisk until combined. Make a well in the dry mix, add the wet ingredients, dates and walnuts and stir until it just starts to come together. If the dough feels too dry, add more crème fraîche, 1 tablespoon (15 ml) at a time. If the dough is too wet, add more flour, 1 tablespoon (8 g) at a time.

Tip the scone mix onto a lightly floured countertop, and gently push the dough together until it's smoother. Knead only a couple of times. The less you work the dough, the better. Shape and press into a round with your hands or gently roll with a rolling pin until the dough is 1½ inches (4 cm) thick. Dip a 2¼-inch (6-cm) cookie cutter in flour and press out the scones (don't twist the cutter). Gather any scraps together and knead lightly. Repeat to form more scones. Place the rounds on your prepared baking sheet so that the scones sit next to one another with just a little space between each of them. Brush the tops of the scones with milk, and bake for 15 to 20 minutes, or until risen and golden brown on top and when tapped, the scones sound hollow in the middle. Serve warm or at room temperature with a generous dollop of thickened cream swirled with honey. These are best eaten on the same day but can be stored in an airtight container for 1 to 2 days.

TEATIME TREAT SPICED PLUM AND HAZELNUT FRIANDS

Yield: **12 friands**

You'd think that I knew of these from my French background, but I actually became aware of friands when living in Australia. These almond-based, light-as-air cakes are incredibly popular in the cafés and bakeries around Australia and New Zealand. It only took me leaving Australia to finally develop my own recipe for these. Instead of almonds I've used ground hazelnuts. I spiced the dough with ginger, nutmeg and cinnamon and topped my friands with sliced plums. The result is a nutty, flavor packed bite that will leave you hooked and coming back for more.

¾ cup (170 g) unsalted butter, divided

¾ cup (100 g) all-purpose flour, plus extra to dust

6 large egg whites

1¾ cups (210 g) confectioners' sugar, plus extra to dust

1¼ cups (120 g) ground hazelnuts

1 cup (115 g) chopped toasted hazelnuts, divided

2 tsp (4 g) ground ginger

1 tsp nutmeg

1 tsp cinnamon

½ tsp salt

6 oz (170 g) pitted and thinly sliced plums (about 3 plums)

Preheat the oven to 350°F (180°C). Melt the butter in a small skillet. Lightly grease the inside of each hole of the friand pan with a little of the melted butter and place in the fridge for 5 to 10 minutes so that the butter has a chance to harden up. Set the rest of the butter aside for use later. Remove the pan from the fridge and dust the inside of each hole with a little flour, knocking out the excess.

Place the egg whites in the bowl of an electric stand mixer fitted with the whisk attachment, and whisk until soft peaks form, about 5 minutes. In a large bowl, sift the flour and confectioners' sugar. Add the ground hazelnuts, half of the chopped hazelnuts, ginger, nutmeg, cinnamon and salt and mix well. Stir the remaining melted butter into the flour mixture and mix until just combined. It will be lumpy and thick at this point.

Using a large spoon, fold one-quarter of the egg whites into the flour mixture to lighten it, and then fold in the remainder until just combined. Divide the batter among the friand holes, filling to three-quarters full. Sprinkle with the remaining chopped hazelnuts, and then arrange the plum slices on top of each friand.

Bake for 18 to 20 minutes, or until golden and a toothpick inserted into the center comes out clean. Cool in the pan for 5 minutes, and then run a sharp, pointy knife around the edges of the friands to loosen any stubborn edges before turning them out onto a wire rack to cool completely. Lightly dust with a little confectioners' sugar prior to serving. These are best eaten warm on the day they are made. They can be stored in an airtight container for up to 2 days.

Tip: If you don't have friand pan, a standard cupcake pan will work just as well.

CHOCOLATE ORANGE HAZELNUT BAKLAVA

Yield: 1 (9 x 13-inch [23 x 33-cm]) baklava (40 servings)

Over 15 years ago, when my husband and I lived in Putney, London, we would walk across Putney Bridge to a Middle Eastern café called Café Aziz. Here the glass cabinets were filled with sweet delicacies that we'd enjoy over a coffee, and baklava was one of them. This baklava is without a doubt an impressive way to end a meal, especially served alongside coffee. The indulgent chocolate melts around the chopped hazelnuts and orange in between crispy, buttery phyllo layers. All this gets soaked in an orange syrup resulting in a sticky sweet snack that you'll be returning to for "just one more piece!" These are most definitely worth the effort.

2 (1-lb [454-g]) packages phyllo pastry sheets (26 sheets)

For the Chocolate Hazelnut Filling
3 cups (345 g) whole toasted hazelnuts, skins removed and cooled

2 cups (300 g) 70% dark chocolate

2 tsp (6 g) ground cinnamon

¼ tsp salt

Zest of 1 large orange

1 cup (230 g) unsalted butter

If frozen, thaw the phyllo pastry overnight in the fridge. Then allow the phyllo to come to room temperature on the counter for 1 hour.

To make the chocolate hazelnut filling, add the hazelnuts, chocolate, cinnamon, salt and orange zest to the canister of a food processor. Pulse until the hazelnuts and chocolate are finely chopped to the size of a lentil. Melt the butter in a small saucepan over low heat.

Lay the phyllo sheets flat on top of one another on the counter. Using the base of a 9 x 13–inch (23 x 33–cm) baking dish as a guide, trim the pastry so that it fits snuggly into the base of the dish, keeping any trimmings. Lay a damp tea towel over the pastry sheets to prevent them from drying out.

Brush the base and sides of the baking dish with the melted butter, and lay your first sheet of phyllo across the base. If the sheets aren't quite big enough, cut a strip from the trimmings and fill in the gap. If the phyllo pastry tears at any point, just use your fingers to put it back into place and patch it up. Brush this sheet all over with butter. Lay another phyllo sheet on top and brush with butter again, and keep layering like this until you have 8 sheets of phyllo layered one on top of the other and each one brushed with butter. Spread one-third of the chocolate-nut mixture across the pastry and press it down with the back of a spoon.

Cover with 5 more sheets of buttered phyllo. Spread another third of the chocolate-hazelnut mixture and level. Cover with 5 more sheets of phyllo, buttering each layer. Spread the remaining chocolate hazelnut mixture and top with the remaining phyllo (8 sheets), again, buttering each layer. Pour the remaining butter onto the pastry and brush all over. Refrigerate for 30 minutes to allow the butter to set.

Preheat the oven to 350°F (180°C).

(continued)

For the Orange Syrup

1 cup (240 ml) water

1 cup (200 g) granulated sugar

½ cup (120 ml) honey

½ cup (120 ml) fresh orange juice

Zest of 1 large orange

1 cinnamon stick

Tip: Stir in 2 tablespoons (30 ml) of orange liqueur to the orange syrup just before pouring over the baklava for a boozy kick.

Remove the baking dish from the fridge, and using a large, very sharp knife, cut the baklava into portion-sized pieces to suit. To do this, cut it lengthways into four evenly sized strips and then the same again widthways into five strips, leaving you with 20 squares. Cut each square diagonally into triangles. Make sure that you cut right through to the bottom layer. Bake for 45 minutes to 1 hour, or until the top is golden brown. If the top of the baklava gets too brown, tent it with aluminum foil.

While the baklava is baking, make the orange syrup. Add the water, sugar, honey, orange juice, orange zest and cinnamon stick to a saucepan over medium heat, and bring the liquid to a simmer, stirring until the sugar has dissolved. Increase the heat to medium-high, and boil for 10 to 15 minutes, or until the mixture is syrupy. If you prefer not to have grated zest on your baklava, use orange peel instead. Remove from the heat and set aside. When the baklava has finished baking, remove the tray from the oven. Discard the cinnamon stick (and orange peel if applicable) from the syrup, and then spoon the syrup over the baklava, making sure that the whole thing gets coated. Run a sharp knife through the previous cuts to ensure that the individual pieces can be easily removed later. Set aside to cool completely and soak up the syrup, approximately 4 to 6 hours. Do not cover while cooling or the phyllo pastry will turn soggy. Baklava can be kept at room temperature for up to 2 weeks tightly wrapped in plastic wrap.

Notes: The layering looks like this:

8 phyllo sheets, brushed with butter between each sheet, and then ⅓ cup chocolate hazelnut mixture

5 phyllo sheets, brushed with butter between each sheet, and then ⅓ cup chocolate hazelnut

5 phyllo sheets, brushed with butter between each sheet, and then ⅓ cup chocolate hazelnut

8 phyllo sheets, brushed with butter between each sheet and also buttered on top of the final sheet

= 26 layers of phyllo pastry in total

Be careful what type of chocolate you use in this recipe. It has to be able to melt. Some baking chocolate will maintain its shape and never melt when baked. This recipe calls for the chocolate in the recipe to melt to coat the hazelnut mixture and help stick the sheets of pastry together. I use either Lindt or Callebaut chocolate.

AUSSIE STRAWBERRY AND LEMON LAMINGTONS

Yield: **16 lamingtons**

Ah, the good ol' Aussie lamington. So classically Australian. I think I made a batch for every school bake sale at my girls' school in Sydney. There are various takes on the lamington where the sponge square is left whole and coated in chocolate icing and shredded coconut or sliced and layered with jam and even piped with whipped cream. My take goes all out for summery goodness by combining the magic of strawberry jam and coconut with a dollop of tangy lemon curd and freshly whipped cream. Pure delight!

For the Lamington Sponge

1¼ cups (250 g) granulated sugar

Zest of 2 large lemons

1 cup (230 g) unsalted butter, room temperature

3 large eggs, room temperature

2 cups (250 g) self-rising flour

1 tsp baking powder

½ tsp salt

⅓ cup (80 ml) fresh lemon juice (about 2 lemons)

Preheat the oven to 350°F (180°C). Grease a 9 x 9–inch (23 x 23–cm) baking pan and line with parchment paper. Allow the parchment paper to hang over the sides to make it easier to lift the sponge out once cooked.

To make the lamington sponge, in a small bowl, combine the sugar and lemon zest, and using your fingertips, rub the two together for 1 minute to release the oils of the zest into the sugar. In the bowl of an electric stand mixer fitted with the paddle attachment, cream the butter and lemon and sugar mixture on medium speed for 5 minutes, or until pale. Add the eggs one at a time, beating until combined between each addition. Ensure that you scrape down the sides of the bowl.

In a separate bowl, sift the flour, baking powder and salt and mix. Add half of the dry ingredients to the batter and mix on low until just combined. Add the lemon juice, and mix again until just incorporated. Add the remaining dry ingredients and fold through until only a couple of streaks remain, being careful not to overmix.

Pour the batter into the prepared dish, and level with an offset spatula. Bake for 40 to 45 minutes, or until the center of the cake springs back up if gently pressed and an inserted toothpick comes out clean. Remove the cake from the oven and cool in the dish for 5 to 10 minutes before turning it out on a wire rack and allowing to cool completely. Once cooled, freeze the sponge for 30 to 45 minutes until it has firmed up, but not enough to freeze solid. Trim the cake edges with a serrated knife, and then cut into 16 squares.

(continued)

For the Coating

1½ cups (480 g) smooth strawberry jam

3 tbsp (45 ml) water

2½ cups (225 g) shredded coconut

For the Filling

1 cup (240 ml) heavy cream

1 cup (240 ml) lemon curd, store-bought

To prepare the jam coating, in a small saucepan over low heat, gently warm the jam and water and stir to combine. Place the coconut in a bowl. Skewer a square of cake with a fork, and holding it over the saucepan of jam, spoon the jam over the cake square until all sides are coated. (Use a pastry brush if it's easier.) Place the square in the bowl of coconut, and roll until completely coated, and then place on a baking sheet lined with parchment paper. Repeat with all the cake squares, and then cover the tray with plastic wrap and refrigerate for 2 hours. This allows the jam to set, making it easier to handle later on.

To make the filling, use an electric hand mixer to beat the cream in a bowl until firm peaks form. Spoon the cream into a piping bag fitted with a ½-inch (1.3-cm) star nozzle. Use a serrated knife to cut the lamington squares in half.

To assemble, spread 2 teaspoons (10 ml) of lemon curd on one cut side of a lamington. Pipe cream onto the lemon curd. Top with the remaining lamington half. Place carefully on a tray. Repeat the process with the remaining lamington halves, curd and cream. Place the tray in the fridge for 30 minutes to set the cream. Serve immediately. These can be stored in an airtight container in the fridge for up to 3 days.

BLACKBERRY-GLAZED BRIOCHE DONUTS

Yield: **10-12** *donuts plus holes*

Donuts, donuts, donuts . . . a classic childhood favorite! (Well, let's be honest, an adult favorite, too.) Whether a sugar-coated ball filled with fruity jam or a ring covered in a sweet glaze, I have many a memory of licking my fingers after devouring a donut! I adore making enriched brioche dough, as it's so versatile in what you can create with it. Donuts are one such example. That golden, crunchy exterior that hides beneath it a soft, pillowy, rich dough is pure heaven. I've topped these with a blackberry glaze. I love to use berries to naturally color a glaze. Would you look at how vibrant it is! It works so well on top of these beauties.

For the Brioche Dough

2¼ tsp (10 g) active dry yeast

¾ cup plus 4 tsp (200 ml) whole milk, lukewarm

⅓ cup (65 g) granulated sugar, divided

4 cups (500 g) all-purpose flour

1 tsp salt

2 large eggs, room temperature

2 tsp (10 ml) vanilla bean paste or extract

½ cup (115 g) unsalted butter, room temperature, cut into cubes

8 cups (2 L) canola oil or sunflower oil for deep frying

To make the brioche dough, add the yeast, milk, and 1 tablespoon (15 g) of the sugar to the bowl of an electric stand mixer and mix well. Set aside for 15 minutes, or until foamy. Add the flour, remaining sugar, salt, eggs and vanilla, and using the dough hook, mix on low for 5 minutes, or until the dough comes together. While the mixer is running on low speed, add the butter gradually, and once incorporated, turn the mixer up to medium speed and knead for 10 minutes. The dough should be pulling away from the sides of the bowl and have formed a "tornado" around the dough hook. Do the windowpane test on the dough by grabbing a small piece of dough in between your fingers and thumbs and stretching it out. If it tears quickly, the dough requires more kneading. If it stretches thinly and you can see the light through it, it's perfect! Tip the dough onto a greased countertop and knead a couple of times until the dough forms a smooth ball. Place the dough ball in a greased bowl and cover with plastic wrap. Let it rise in a warm place for 1½ hours, or until doubled in size.

Knock the air out of the dough by kneading it gently about six or seven times until it turns into a smooth ball. Then roll out on a lightly floured countertop until ¾-inch (2-cm) thick. Leave to rest on the counter for a couple of minutes so the rolled dough can settle. Meanwhile, cut 10 to 12 (4-inch [10-cm]) square pieces of parchment paper, grease their tops lightly with cooking oil spray and arrange them on two baking sheets.

Using a 3-inch (7.5-cm) round cutter coated in flour (or a drinking glass), cut out rounds from the dough. Then cut out smaller holes with a 1-inch (2.5-cm) round cutter in the middle. Knead any leftover dough, and reroll it to get more donuts. I cut out lots of donut holes with the scraps from this second round of rolling. Place the donut rings on their individual pieces of greased parchment on the baking sheets, leaving space between each one. Place the donut holes on their own piece or two of parchment as well. Cover the donuts with a slightly damp tea towel. Proof in a warm place for 45 minutes to 1½ hours, or until doubled in size and puffy.

(continued)

For the Blackberry Glaze

1 cup (140 g) fresh or frozen blackberries (don't thaw if using frozen)

1 tbsp (15 ml) fresh lemon juice

2 cups (240 g) confectioners' sugar, plus more if needed

2–3 tbsp (30–45 ml) heavy cream, plus more if needed

1 tbsp (18 g) pearl sugar or sprinkles

Fill a heavy saucepan halfway with the oil. Heat the oil to 340 to 350°F (170 to 180°C) using a candy thermometer to check the temperature accurately. Once it has reached this temperature, turn the heat down to stop it from climbing any further. Then regularly check to ensure the temperature is holding steady. Working with two or three at a time, slide the donuts on their paper into the oil. Use tongs to pluck out the papers, which should float free within seconds. Sliding the doughnuts into the oil on the paper will allow them to hold their shape; otherwise, trying to move them with a spatula might deflate the dough before it hits the oil.

Fry for approximately 2 minutes on each side until golden brown. Remove with a slotted spoon and place on a tray lined with paper towels to drain. Repeat the steps until all the donuts are fried. Don't forget the donut holes, which will take about 30 seconds to fry on each side. Allow the donuts to cool before dipping into the glaze.

To make the blackberry glaze, in a small saucepan over medium heat, combine the blackberries and lemon juice and bring to a simmer. Cook for 5 to 7 minutes, stirring constantly and gently mashing the berries to a pulp with a fork. Remove from the heat. Place a fine-mesh strainer over a small bowl and push the pulp through, leaving any seeds or large chunks behind. Allow the blackberry juice to cool for at least 10 minutes before using. Transfer the blackberry juice to a large bowl, add the confectioners' sugar and cream and whisk until smooth. If the glaze appears too thin, add more confectioners' sugar ¼ cup (30 g) at a time. If the glaze appears too thick, add in a little more cream, 1 teaspoon at a time, until you reach the desired consistency.

Dip each donut in the blackberry glaze, set aside on a wire rack and sprinkle immediately with pearl sugar or sprinkles. Allow the icing to set for 15 minutes. Dip the donut holes in the glaze or toss in caster sugar. These are best eaten straightaway or stored in an airtight container for up to 2 days.

MAPLE-GLAZED APPLE PECAN SCROLLS

Yield: **12** *scrolls*

Maple. Apples. Pecan. My three favorite autumn flavors that work beautifully on their own but come together so well in this recipe. These flavors remind me of going on long, chilly walks on a Sunday morning with the girls running around in fallen leaves and returning home to enjoy these scrolls fresh out of the oven. The soft, pull-apart brioche dough encircles sweet, toffee-like apple pieces and toasty, crunchy pecans. Smothered in a maple glaze with a sprinkle of more chopped pecans, these scrolls are a flavor sensation. I hope this recipe taps into a nostalgic feeling for you too and reminds you of a beautiful time with family or friends.

For the Brioche Dough

2¼ tsp (10 g) active dry yeast

¾ cup plus 4 tsp (200 ml) whole milk, lukewarm

⅓ cup (65 g) granulated sugar, divided

4 cups (500 g) all-purpose flour

1 tsp salt

2 large eggs, room temperature

2 tsp (10 ml) vanilla bean paste or extract

½ cup (115 g) unsalted butter, room temperature, cut into cubes, plus more for greasing

For the Apple Pecan Filling

½ cup (115 g) unsalted butter, softened

2 cups (240 g) peeled, cored and chopped apples (about 2 medium apples)

¾ cup (80 g) roughly chopped toasted pecans

⅔ cup (140 g) firmly packed brown sugar

1 tbsp (8 g) ground cinnamon

To make the brioche dough, add the yeast, milk, and 1 tablespoon (15 g) of the sugar into the bowl of an electric stand mixer and mix well. Set aside for 15 minutes, or until foamy. Add the flour, remaining sugar, salt, eggs and vanilla, and using the dough hook, mix on low for 5 minutes, or until the dough comes together. While the mixer is running on low speed, add the butter gradually, and once incorporated, turn the mixer up to medium speed and knead for 10 minutes. The dough should be pulling away from the sides of the bowl and have formed a "tornado" around the dough hook. Do the windowpane test on the dough by grabbing a small piece of dough in between your fingers and thumbs and stretch it out. If it tears quickly, the dough requires more kneading. If it stretches thinly and you can see the light through it, it's perfect!

Tip the dough onto a greased countertop and pull the corners into the center. Turn over so that the seams are underneath, place the dough ball in a greased bowl and cover with plastic wrap. Let it rise in a warm place for 1½ hours, or until doubled in size. Gently punch down the dough, form into a rectangle and wrap in plastic wrap. Refrigerate it for 2 hours or freeze it for 45 minutes (my preferred option). This step is optional, but chilling the dough now makes it much easier to roll and shape later on.

Grease a 9 x 13–inch (23 x 33–cm) baking dish with butter. Once the dough is cold, on a lightly floured countertop, roll the dough into a rectangle measuring approximately 12 x 18 inches (30 x 46 cm).

For the filling, spoon the softened butter all over the dough rectangle and gently smooth out to the edges. The butter has to be super soft, so as not to tear the dough. If necessary, place in the microwave for 10 seconds or so to soften. But don't melt it! In a medium bowl, mix the apples, pecans, brown sugar and cinnamon, and sprinkle evenly all over the butter.

(continued)

For the Maple Glaze

1½ cups (180 g) confectioners' sugar

3 tbsp (45 ml) pure maple syrup

1 tbsp (15 ml) whole milk

⅓ cup (35 g) chopped toasted pecans, to decorate

Starting at the long side of the dough rectangle, roll the dough tightly into a log, and then pinch the seam closed with your fingers. Using unflavored dental floss or a sharp knife, cut the ends off the roll, as they won't be as filled as the rest of the log. Cut the log into 12 even pieces, about 1½ inches (4 cm) wide. Place the rolls on their sides with their scrolls facing up in the prepared dish. Leave room around each roll. Cover with plastic wrap and let rise in a warm place for 45 minutes until they have expanded by about half of their original volume.

Preheat the oven to 350°F (180°C). Remove the plastic wrap and bake the rolls for 25 to 30 minutes, or until golden brown. Cover with foil about halfway through so as not to brown them too much.

While the rolls are baking, make the maple glaze. In a medium bowl, whisk together the confectioners' sugar, maple syrup and milk, until smooth. When the rolls are finished baking, let them cool for about 10 minutes. Drizzle the frosting over the cinnamon rolls, using the back of a spoon to spread if desired. Sprinkle with chopped pecans and serve. These are best served on the same day but can be stored at room temperature in an airtight container for up to 3 days or in the fridge for up to 5 days.

Notes: To toast the pecans, place the pecans on a baking sheet, and bake in a 350°F (180°C) oven for 10 to 15 minutes, or until they smell nice and toasty and are a shade or two darker.

You can easily turn these into overnight scrolls. Once the dough is filled with the apple mixture, rolled, sliced and placed in the prepared pan, wrap the pan tightly in plastic wrap and refrigerate overnight. The next morning, remove from the fridge and let sit at room temperature for 45 minutes before baking per the instructions.

FAVORITE CHILDHOOD FROZEN TREATS

This has got to be the most fun chapter in the book! I mean, we all have our favorite frozen treats from childhood, right? Whether it's Strawberry Shortcake Popsicles (page 147) that had you running after the ice cream truck or a triple scoop of Chocolate Hazelnut Gelato with Fudge Sauce (page 158), I've got you covered.

While I was developing these recipes, I enjoyed thinking about the different ways that we can make ice cream and including those variations here, such as Tropical Mango and Coconut Froyo (page 148). It's a super-simple way of making ice cream: freezing the fruit and then blending in a food processor to create this mouth-wateringly beautiful frozen yogurt. Pass me my sunglasses! I'm on holiday every time I eat this.

No-churn ice creams are a staple of every family's freezer drawer as they are just so easy to make. In my Kids' Fave Neapolitan No-Churn Ice Cream (page 157), you have the three familiar flavors of strawberry, vanilla and chocolate in the one dish—every kid's dream!

For the gelato connoisseurs, I've got your back. I thoroughly enjoy the process of making custard-based ice creams, as the results are just heavenly. The Off-to-the-Movies Caramel Popcorn Choc-Tops (page 161) combine an incredible caramel gelato, scooped into a waffle cone, dipped in dark chocolate and topped with crunchy caramel popcorn. Who needs to go to the cinema when you can enjoy these at home!

STRAWBERRY SHORTCAKE POPSICLES

Yield: **8–10** *popsicles*

Here we have an American childhood staple sold in ice cream trucks and corner stores and loved by school kids. This is my spin on the nostalgic classic using a no-churn base to create a flavorsome strawberry ice cream drizzled with white chocolate and topped with a delicious strawberry shortcake crumble. Need I say more?

For the Strawberry Ice Cream

1½ cups (250 g) hulled and sliced fresh ripe strawberries

3 tbsp (60 g) strawberry jam

1 tbsp (15 g) granulated sugar

1 tsp vanilla extract

¼ tsp salt

¾ cup (180 ml) condensed milk

½ cup (120 g) cream cheese, room temperature

½ cup (120 ml) heavy cream

For the Strawberry Shortcake Crumb

½ cup (70 g) shortcake biscuits or vanilla sandwich cookies

1 tsp unsalted butter

½ cup (10 g) freeze-dried strawberries

For the White Chocolate Drizzle

⅔ cup (100 g) finely chopped white chocolate

To make the strawberry ice cream, in a blender, add the strawberries, strawberry jam, sugar, vanilla and salt, and blend until smooth. Pour the strawberry purée into a medium bowl. It makes about 1 cup (240 ml). Add the condensed milk and cream cheese, and using an electric hand mixer on high, beat well for 2 minutes, or until aerated.

In a separate bowl, beat the cream on high speed until stiff peaks form. Add one-quarter of the whipped cream to the strawberry mixture, and fold through until combined. Add the remaining whipped cream and fold through gently until evenly distributed. Divide the mixture into popsicle molds, filling them to just below the top, leaving some room for the ice cream to expand. Insert wooden sticks and freeze until completely firm, about 6 hours or overnight. Once set, remove the popsicles from their molds, place on a baking sheet lined with parchment paper and return to the freezer.

To make the strawberry shortcake crumb, pulse the cookies in a food processor until fine crumbs form. Melt the butter in a skillet. Add the butter and freeze-dried strawberries to the food processor, and pulse a few times to create strawberry crumbs.

To make the drizzle, gently melt the white chocolate in the microwave in 20-second intervals at half power, stirring as you go. Allow to cool slightly. Remove the popsicles on their tray from the freezer and drizzle as much white chocolate as you like over each, and then instantly sprinkle the strawberry shortcake crumb over the top so it sticks to the white chocolate. Work quickly as the white chocolate will set! Return the popsicles to the freezer until you're ready to serve. Any leftover strawberry shortcake crumb can be used to top ice cream, yogurt or cupcakes! These will keep in the freezer for up to 2 weeks. Wrap individually in plastic wrap to protect them from freezer burn.

Tip: You will most likely have leftover white chocolate coating, and one idea is to make strawberry white chocolate bark out of it. To do this, pour the remaining white chocolate out onto a piece of parchment paper and sprinkle freeze-dried strawberries or any remaining strawberry shortcake crumb over the top. Refrigerate until set, and break into pieces.

TROPICAL MANGO AND COCONUT FROYO

*Yield: **6 servings***

This is possibly the easiest of all the recipes in this chapter, and it's a flavor sensation. Mangoes have been my favorite fruit since my days visiting my parents on school holidays when they lived in New Delhi. I adore their fragrant sweetness, succulent juiciness and rich texture. All this combined with coconut and lime in a soft serve–style froyo makes for a tropical whirlwind of flavor. I guarantee you'll go back for more than one serving, it's that easy to eat!

4 cups (680 g) fresh ripe mango flesh

1 cup (240 ml) full-fat plain Greek yogurt

½ cup (120 ml) coconut milk

½ cup (120 ml) honey

1 tbsp (15 ml) fresh lime juice

Zest of 1 large lime

Mint leaves

Toasted coconut flakes

Dried mango, sliced (optional)

In a high-powered blender or the canister of a food processor add the mangoes, Greek yogurt, coconut milk, honey, lime juice and zest and process until smooth. Pour into a freezer-safe, airtight container, and freeze until solid, up to 6 hours or overnight. Tip: It's easier to break up the frozen yogurt in the next step if the container is shallow rather than deep.

When ready to serve, remove the mango frozen yogurt from the freezer and break it up into chunks with a fork. Place in a high-powered blender or food processor and blend until smooth. Serve immediately in bowls for a soft-serve consistency, and garnish with a combination of mint leaves, coconut flakes and dried mango (if using). Leftovers can be poured back into the freezer-safe container and frozen until solid. Scoop out as desired. This recipe can easily be doubled for twice the deliciousness.

Tip: Store-bought frozen mango can be used to replace fresh mango. However, my experience is that this mango is extremely tart rather than sweet, and you may have to increase the quantity of honey to compensate. Do not reduce the quantity of honey in the recipe though, as this natural sugar is what stops the frozen yogurt from freezing into a rock-hard block.

RETRO PEACHES 'N' CREAM ARCTIC SLICE

Yield: **14–18** *slices*

Arctic slice . . . what's that? Okay, growing up in the UK, the Arctic roll was every kid's favorite treat. A dessert made of a cylinder of vanilla ice cream surrounded by a layer of raspberry sauce and a thin layer of sponge, this roll filled many a freezer back in the day. While developing this recipe, I came to realize that trying to shape ice cream into a roll and then surrounding it with sponge was tricky, to say the least. So, I transformed it into a slice to make life easier for all of us! I've evolved the simple ice cream by creating a delicious peaches 'n' cream version (equally amazing on its own) and sandwiched it between lemon sponge and raspberry jam. Such a fun take on the retro classic.

For the Peaches 'n' Cream Ice Cream

4 cups (660 g) pitted and sliced ripe yellow peaches (about 6 peaches)

2 cups (480 ml) crème fraîche

¾ cup (180 ml) heavy cream

½ cup (110 g) firmly packed brown sugar

½ cup (100 g) granulated sugar

1 tbsp (15 ml) fresh lemon juice

1 tsp vanilla extract

For the Lemon Sponge

½ cup (100 g) granulated sugar, plus extra for dusting

Zest of 1 large lemon

4 large eggs, room temperature

1 tsp vanilla extract

1 cup (125 g) all-purpose flour

1 tsp baking powder

¼ tsp salt

¾ cup (240 g) raspberry jam, divided

1–2 tbsp (15–30 ml) milk, if needed

For Serving

1 tbsp (8 g) confectioners' sugar, to dust

Whipped cream (optional)

Fresh raspberries (optional)

Fresh peaches, sliced (optional)

To make the peaches 'n' cream ice cream, add the peaches, crème fraîche, cream, brown sugar, granulated sugar, lemon juice and vanilla to the canister of a food processor or a blender and purée until smooth. Scrape into a freezer container, cover with plastic wrap and freeze for 6 hours or overnight.

Two hours before the ice cream has finished hardening in the freezer, make two layers of lemon sponge. Preheat the oven to 375°F (190°C). Grease a 9 x 9–inch (23 x 23–cm) baking pan and line the base and sides with parchment paper.

In a small bowl, combine the sugar and lemon zest, and using your fingertips, rub the two together for 1 minute to release the oils of the zest into the sugar. Next, in the bowl of an electric stand mixer fitted with the paddle attachment, cream the eggs and lemon and sugar mixture on medium speed for 5 minutes, or until pale. Add the vanilla and sift the flour, baking powder and salt over the bowl of the mixer, and then fold together until there are no visible lumps of flour. Carefully pour half of the batter into the prepared baking pan and smooth over the top with an offset spatula. Set aside the remaining batter. Bake for 10 to 12 minutes, or until springy to the touch and golden. When the sponge is cooked, allow it to cool for 2 minutes in the pan, and then flip it upside down onto a piece of parchment paper sprinkled with sugar. Carefully peel off the paper revealing the underside of the sponge and allow to cool completely. Set aside. Re-grease and line the baking pan with parchment paper. This time allow the parchment paper to hang over the sides to make it easier to lift the arctic slice once frozen.

Pour the remaining batter into this pan. Level off and bake for 10 to 12 minutes, or until springy to the touch and golden. Leave this second sponge to cool completely in the pan. (If you have two 9 x 9–inch [23 x 23–cm] baking pans, you can bake both layers of sponge at the same time.) Spoon half of the raspberry jam onto the sponge layer in the pan, and using an offset spatula, smooth it out evenly right up to the edges of the sponge all around.

(continued)

To assemble, remove the peach ice cream from the freezer and allow to stand at room temperature for 15 minutes. Break the frozen ice cream into pieces (with a fork) and process in the food processor until smooth. If your food processor has a hard time processing the chunks initially, add 1 to 2 tablespoons (15 to 30 ml) of milk to help the machine break down the ice cream. The peach ice cream will have a soft-serve consistency. Pour this peach ice cream onto the raspberry jam and sponge base and level with an offset spatula, pushing the ice cream right up to the edges. Spoon the remaining raspberry jam onto the underside of the remaining sponge square, spreading it out evenly and neatly right to the edges. Place the sponge top, flipped over with the jam side facing down onto the ice cream in the pan. Gently press the sponge top down onto the ice cream layer, and then wrap the pan in plastic wrap and freeze for 6 hours minimum.

When ready to serve, use the parchment paper to lift the whole ice cream and sponge square out of the pan onto a chopping board. Dust with confectioners' sugar. Use a large knife to slice the block in half and then each half into 1-inch (2.5-cm)-wide slices. Serve immediately. Optionally, remove one-half of the block and top with whipped cream, fresh raspberries and peach slices before serving. Uneaten slices can be individually wrapped in plastic wrap or baking parchment and refrozen.

BROWNIE PEANUT BUTTER ICE CREAM SANDWICH

Yield: **8–9 large ice cream sandwiches**

This recipe really does feature the best of both worlds. Soft, fudgy brownie cookies and rich, creamy peanut butter ice cream . . . it doesn't get much better than this. The ice cream is no-churn and comes together in minutes. While the ice cream freezes, make your brownie cookies and then sandwich the two components together to make one indulgent treat that you'll be sure to love.

For the Peanut Butter Ice Cream

1 cup (260 g) smooth peanut butter

1 (14-oz [307-ml]) can condensed milk

1 tsp vanilla extract

¼ tsp salt

1½ cups (360 ml) heavy cream

1 cup (150 g) chopped chocolate peanut butter cups (I like Reese's; optional)

To make the peanut butter ice cream, warm the peanut butter in a bowl in the microwave for about 10 to 20 seconds, until it becomes easier to stir but is not piping hot. In the bowl of an electric stand mixer fitted with the whisk attachment, whisk the condensed milk, vanilla and salt for 2 minutes until thicker. Add the peanut butter and beat until combined and aerated. Remove as much off the whisk attachment into the bowl as possible. Set this peanut butter mixture aside.

In a separate bowl of an electric stand mixer (no need to wash the whisk attachment), add the cream, and beat on medium until firm peaks form. Add one-quarter of the whipped cream to the peanut butter mixture and fold through to loosen the mixture. Add the remaining whipped cream and chopped peanut butter cups (if using), and fold through gently until evenly distributed.

Line a 9 x 13–inch (23 x 33–cm) baking dish with parchment paper. (I grease the pan with butter so that the paper sticks to the sides.) Ensure there is an overhang to be able to lift the slab of ice cream out of the pan later. Pour the peanut butter cream mixture into the prepared pan and smooth with an offset spatula. Cover the ice cream with another sheet of parchment paper and freeze for 4 to 6 hours, or until solid.

(continued)

For the Brownie Cookies

1⅔ cups (250 g) coarsely chopped 70% dark chocolate

½ cup (115 g) unsalted butter, room temperature

2 large eggs, room temperature

1½ cups (300 g) firmly packed light brown sugar

1 cup (125 g) spelt flour

¼ cup (30 g) unsweetened cocoa powder

1 tsp baking powder

¼ tsp salt

Natural sea salt flakes, for sprinkling (optional)

Meanwhile, make the brownie cookies. Preheat the oven to 350°F (180°C). Line two baking sheets with parchment paper. Melt the chocolate and butter in a bowl set over a pan of simmering water, ensuring the bottom of the bowl does not come into contact with the water. Allow to cool for 15 minutes.

In the bowl of an electric stand mixer fitted with the whisk attachment, whip the eggs and sugar together on medium speed for 5 minutes, or until pale and creamy. Reduce the mixer speed to low, gradually pour in the melted chocolate and butter and beat until just combined. In a separate bowl, sift the flour, cocoa powder, baking powder and salt. Add the dry ingredients to the mixing bowl and fold through with a rubber spatula until just combined.

Drop one level ice cream scoop of the cookie dough onto the prepared baking sheets, allowing room for spreading. Repeat until you've used up all of the dough. This should make 16 to 18 cookie scoops. Bake for 8 to 10 minutes, or until just firm. The cookies will look set at the edges but still look a little wet in the center. Don't overbake or the cookies won't be crackly and fudgy. Remove from the oven and give the pan a firm tap on your countertop. Then, with a cookie cutter slightly larger than the cookie, hula hoop the cookie cutter around each cookie so that the cookie gets gently pushed into a circle. Sprinkle with flaky salt, if using. Set aside on the trays to cool for 10 minutes, and then transfer to a wire rack to cool completely. Refrigerate for 30 minutes until ready to assemble.

To serve, match the cookies up in size so that you have a top and bottom cookie for each sandwich. Remove the peanut butter ice cream from the freezer, and lift the ice cream slab from the tray using the parchment paper. Using a cookie cutter about the same diameter as the cookies, punch out rounds of ice cream. To make each sandwich, place one round of ice cream between two cookies and gently squeeze together. Return the sandwiches to the freezer for 1 hour before serving. Leftover ice cream can be spooned into an airtight container and frozen.

Tips: For smaller sandwiches, use a smaller ice cream scoop to make the cookies smaller or slice the ice cream sandwiches in half when serving.

You can use all-purpose flour instead of spelt flour.

KIDS' FAVE NEAPOLITAN NO-CHURN ICE CREAM

Yield: **8 *servings***

Opening that tub to reveal three delicious and instantly recognizable flavors of strawberry, vanilla and chocolate make Neapolitan ice cream a firm favorite dessert for kids. My version uses a no-churn ice cream base to keep this as simple as possible to make. The hardest part is choosing whether to enjoy a scoop in a waffle cone or multiple scoops in a bowl. It's delicious!

1 cup (160 g) diced fresh strawberries

3 tbsp (60 g) strawberry jam

2 tbsp (10 g) unsweetened cocoa powder

1 (14-oz [307-ml]) can condensed milk

2 tsp (10 ml) vanilla extract

¼ tsp salt

2 cups (480 ml) heavy cream

2–4 drops natural red food coloring (optional)

Freeze-dried strawberries (optional)

Meringue kisses, crushed (optional)

Dark chocolate, grated (optional)

Place three equal-sized bowls on your counter. In the first one, place your diced strawberries and jam and mash together. In the second bowl, add the cocoa powder. One bowl will be remaining empty for the moment.

In the bowl of an electric stand mixer fitted with the paddle attachment, beat the condensed milk, vanilla and salt for 2 minutes until thickened. Divide the condensed milk mixture equally between the three bowls.

In the bowl of the electric stand mixer (no need to wash it), add the cream and beat on medium speed until firm peaks form. Divide the whipped cream between the three bowls, adding a ⅓ cup (80 ml) less to the strawberry bowl than the other two, as the strawberries add bulk to the mixture. Gently fold the contents of each bowl separately so that you're left with a strawberry mixture, chocolate mixture and vanilla mixture. Add in a few drops of natural red food coloring to the strawberry mixture if you'd like a more vibrant pink color. The chocolate mixture is the thickest of the three due to the cocoa powder and will hold its shape well. Regarding the vanilla mixture, once combined, if it has lost its firm dollop consistency, add it back into the bowl of the stand mixer and beat again until firm peaks return.

In a 9 x 5–inch (23 x 13–cm) loaf pan (you can line it with parchment paper if you like), spoon the chocolate mixture first into one-third of the pan. Next, spoon the vanilla mixture into the middle of the pan, and lastly, spoon the strawberry mixture into the final third. Sprinkle with freeze-dried strawberries over the strawberry section, crushed meringue kisses over the vanilla section and grated chocolate over the chocolate section, if using. Cover with plastic wrap and freeze for 4 to 6 hours or until solid. Remove 10 to 15 minutes before serving to soften slightly.

Tip: If your mixtures are too runny to be able to dollop next to each other in the loaf pan, cut rectangles of thin cardboard or cardstock, wrap them in plastic wrap and use them as dividers. Pour the mixtures into their slots, then slowly pull the dividers out prior to freezing. Alternatively, layer the three mixtures by spooning the chocolate into the bottom and leveling it out. Then spoon the vanilla on top and level out, followed by the strawberry layer.

CHOCOLATE HAZELNUT GELATO WITH FUDGE SAUCE

*Yield: **6 servings***

This one's for the ice cream aficionados out there. Those who appreciate the process of making the custard base in order to churn it in an ice cream maker, resulting in a rich, indulgent, and most importantly, creamy chocolate hazelnut gelato. This gelato is for you, and it is delectable. In addition to the beautiful nutty, milk-chocolate gelato, I created a fudge sauce to pour over the top. Let's take this to a whole other level, shall we?

For the Chocolate Hazelnut Gelato

2 cups (240 g) whole hazelnuts

2 cups (480 ml) whole milk

1¼ cups (300 ml) heavy cream

5 large egg yolks, room temperature

½ cup (100 g) granulated sugar

Preheat the oven to 350°F (180°C).

To make the chocolate hazelnut gelato, spread the hazelnuts on a baking sheet and toast in the oven for 8 to 10 minutes, or until lightly golden brown. Stir them halfway through so that they toast evenly. Let them cool completely, and then rub them with a paper towel to remove as much of the skins as possible. Place the nuts in the canister of a food processor and pulse until finely chopped. Alternatively, place the nuts into a resealable plastic storage bag and crush with a rolling pin.

Combine the milk and chopped hazelnuts in a medium saucepan over medium heat. Once the mixture starts steaming, just before it starts to boil, remove the pan from the heat, cover with a lid and let steep for 2 hours. Pass through a fine-meshed sieve into a clean saucepan, pressing hard on the solids to squeeze out as much of the milk as you can. Reserve the strained milk and discard the solids.

In this saucepan, add the cream to the hazelnut milk, and heat gently over medium-low heat. Heat until the milk is steaming and bubbles appear around the side of the pan just before boiling. Meanwhile, in a medium bowl, use a whisk to whip the egg yolks with the sugar until the eggs have become thick and pale yellow. While continuously whisking, slowly pour the hot milk and cream into the egg mixture. Pour the egg mixture back into the saucepan, and while whisking continuously, cook over medium heat until the mixture thickens and coats the back of a spoon.

(continued)

1 cup (150 g) finely chopped milk chocolate

½ cup (150 g) chocolate hazelnut spread

1 tsp vanilla extract

1 tbsp (15 ml) hazelnut liqueur, such as Frangelico (optional)

For the Fudge Sauce

½ cup (100 g) granulated sugar

1 (12-oz [354-ml]) can evaporated milk

¼ cup (60 g) unsalted butter

1 cup (150 g) coarsely chopped 70% dark chocolate

1 tsp vanilla extract

For Serving (optional)

Waffle cones, store-bought

Toasted hazelnuts, crushed

Place the milk chocolate, chocolate hazelnut spread, vanilla and hazelnut liquor, if using, into a bowl. Pour the custard mixture through a fine-mesh sieve into the bowl. Let it sit for a couple of minutes, and then mix vigorously, scraping the melted chocolate off the bottom. It may take a couple of minutes to fully incorporate the chocolate. Place a piece of plastic wrap on the surface of the custard to prevent a skin from forming. Chill this mixture completely in the fridge, and then pour into the frozen cylinder of your ice cream maker and follow the manufacturer's instructions to freeze. Spoon the mixture into a freezer-safe container, place a piece of parchment paper on the surface, and freeze for 4 to 6 hours, or until solid.

To make the chocolate fudge sauce, place the sugar, evaporated milk, butter, dark chocolate and vanilla in a medium saucepan over medium heat. Bring to a boil, stirring constantly, and then heat for 5 minutes until thickened. Remove from the heat and allow to cool slightly. It will thicken as it cools. To get it to a pouring consistency, heat the sauce in 10-second bursts in the microwave. The sauce can be stored in an airtight container in the fridge for up to 1 month.

When ready to serve, remove the gelato from the freezer and allow to soften for 15 minutes. Using an ice cream scoop dipped in boiling water, scoop out gelato into a waffle cone (if using), pour your desired amount of chocolate fudge sauce over the top and sprinkle with chopped hazelnuts (if using). Eat immediately!

Tip: Dip the open end of your cone into the fudge sauce, and then into the chopped hazelnuts for extra taste!

OFF-TO-THE-MOVIES CARAMEL POPCORN CHOC-TOPS

Yield: 10 *choc-tops*

Here's another chance to make traditional-style gelato, this time flavored with caramel sauce to form the ice cream and also to swirl throughout. This is reminiscent of the days visiting the cinema and enjoying a choc-top ice cream. For those who have never enjoyed this delightful treat, a choc-top is traditionally one scoop of vanilla ice cream placed in a small waffle cone and coated with a hardened chocolate shell. There was nothing better than one of these simple, delicious pleasures as a kid. Here's the chance to recreate this at home by encasing a scoop of caramel gelato in a waffle cone in dark chocolate and topping it off with crunchy caramel popcorn.

For the Caramel Gelato

1 cup (200 g) granulated sugar

½ cup (115 g) unsalted butter, room temperature and chopped

2 cups (480 ml) heavy cream, room temperature, divided

1 tsp vanilla bean paste

2 tsp (12 g) natural sea salt flakes, or to taste

2 cups (480 ml) whole milk

4 large egg yolks, room temperature

½ cup (110 g) firmly packed brown sugar

To make the caramel gelato, first prepare the caramel so that it has time to cool slightly while making the ice cream custard base. In a high-sided nonstick saucepan, heat the granulated sugar over medium heat, stirring often with a wooden spoon. Once the sugar is in liquid form, stop stirring and just swirl the liquid sugar as the color changes to a lovely amber. Keep an eagle eye on it at this stage as it can turn to burnt sugar very quickly. It will bubble up, but whisk the butter in until it has thoroughly melted. Then remove from the heat. Add ¾ cup (180 ml) of the cream. Again, it will bubble, but keep whisking and the bubbling will die down. Return it to medium heat, stirring occasionally, so that the caramel can thicken. This takes about 5 minutes. Remove from the heat, stir in the vanilla bean paste and sea salt, to taste, and set aside in the pan while you make the gelato custard base.

In a saucepan over medium-low heat, add the milk and the remaining cream, and heat gently until the milk is steaming and bubbles appear around the side of the pan just before boiling. Meanwhile, in a medium bowl, whip the egg yolks and brown sugar with a whisk until the eggs have become thick and pale yellow. While continuously whisking, slowly pour the hot milk and cream over the top of the yolks and whisk until combined. Return all the mixture to the saucepan, and while whisking constantly, cook over medium heat until the mixture thickens and coats the back of a spoon. Pour the custard mixture through a fine-mesh sieve into a bowl, and then add three-quarters of the caramel and mix until combined. Place a piece of plastic wrap on the surface of the gelato to prevent a skin from forming.

(continued)

For Serving

2 cups (300 g) finely chopped
54% dark chocolate

1 tbsp (15 ml) coconut oil

10 small waffle cones, store-bought

1½ cups (185 g) caramel popcorn,
store-bought

Chill the mixture completely in the fridge, and then pour into the frozen cylinder of an ice cream maker and follow the manufacturer's instructions to freeze. Spoon the mixture into a freezer-safe container, pour in the remaining caramel and swirl through, taking care not to overmix. Place a piece of parchment paper on the surface and freeze until firm, 4 hours minimum. Remove from the freezer and scoop out single balls of ice cream, placing them on a baking sheet lined with parchment paper. Place back into the freezer until ready to serve.

When you're ready to assemble the cones, prepare the choc-top coating. Place the chocolate and coconut oil in a microwaveable bowl and mix to combine. Microwave in 30-second bursts, stirring periodically until the chocolate is smooth and melted. Pour the melted mixture into a container that is just wide enough to fit your cones. (I used a drinking glass.) Cool slightly if it is hot, stirring occasionally.

Working one cone at a time, scoop one of your balls of ice cream and pack it gently but firmly into the cone. Dip the cone, gelato-end first, into the chocolate mixture, making sure to fully immerse the gelato. Quickly remove the gelato from the chocolate, letting any excess drip off, and immediately sprinkle on the caramel popcorn. Place the cone into a glass to keep it upright, and wait for 1 to 2 minutes for the chocolate to set. Lay the cone back onto the baking sheet, and pop it into the freezer straight away. Repeat this process until all the gelato and cones are used up.

Serve immediately, but if the gelato has softened, allow time in the freezer to harden up. Individually wrap each cone in plastic wrap if not serving straight away.

Tip: Gelato can be served directly in bowls. Dark chocolate can be drizzled over the top.

ACKNOWLEDGMENTS

Through a global pandemic, when everything around us was changing daily, it was my beautiful family who believed in me and said YES to jumping on this cookbook project. I internally freaked out about how I would manage it all, but you maintained faith in me.

Anthony, you provided that calming voice that let me know everything was possible. Thank you for your unwavering belief in me and for knowing what I'm able to achieve, sometimes even before I knew it myself. Thank you for cooking dinner every night, realizing that after 10 hours of recipe testing, the kitchen was the last place I wanted to be! Thank you for heading to the shops at all hours to pick up one more block of butter, one more bag of sugar or one more bar of chocolate.

To my girls Malia, Lani and Coco. Having to invest so much of myself came at the price of time spent with you. Not ideal when we were all at home together so much during such a strange year. But you patiently allowed me to disappear into the kitchen for hours on end or wave my camera around as you talked to me. I hope that this book forms part of your baking journey so that in the years to come you can pick it up, flick through and remember the time Mum made a cookbook!

To Page Street Publishing, and Emily in particular, thank you for seeing potential in me, so soon in my career, and encouraging me to write, develop and photograph this book. Your email landed in my inbox the same week that the world shut itself into lockdown as the pandemic took over and my client work halted. It was one of those sliding-door moments where one side of my business closed (temporarily), but another opportunity opened up. These past six months have propelled me creatively like I would never have believed. I've become a better developer, stylist and photographer because of it.

To my army of recipe testers, I am humbled by your generosity in raising your hand to test my recipes. Through a callout on social media, I ended up with fifty-four testers across the globe who each took it upon themselves to test and provide invaluable feedback. This food community blows me away daily as, above all, it's supportive of one another. You showed that support in spades. Thank you.

And lastly, thank you to the readers of my blog, Emma Duckworth Bakes, and my Instagram community who have made this all possible. This is still a relatively new career for me, and I still have pinch-me moments where I can't believe that I'm here with my own cookbook, where every word, every recipe and every image is my own. Through all the likes and comments, you've enabled me to develop enough of a presence on social media to get noticed by a publishing house. Wow! Thank you.

Through all the connections I've made on this food photography journey, I've made some real friendships with peers in my industry. In no particular order, Deb, Michele, Anna, Ana, Anja, Erin, Sarah, Ari, Mike, Kelsey, Sabine, Roberta, Sam, LeAnne and Dee, I admire you all. From your answers to the random questions that I throw out, to the words of wisdom and support, I appreciate all of your guidance and encouragement. Your talents astound me and constantly make me strive to be a better creative.

ABOUT THE AUTHOR

Emma Duckworth is a London-based recipe developer, food stylist and food photographer. She creates and develops sweet treats and desserts for her own website, www.emmaduckworthbakes.co.uk and her Instagram channel @emmaduckworthbakes. She also works with brands through recipe development and content creation, having worked with Waitrose, Sainsbury's, Nielsen-Massey Vanillas, Bonne Maman and Lyle's Golden Syrup, to name a few. Her work has been featured in *Bake from Scratch* magazine, *sisterMAG*, Purely Elizabeth, feedfeed and *eat.live.escape* magazine. Emma continues to perfect her food styling and photography while creating inspiration for others to jump into the kitchen and bake.

INDEX